Moments
of
Presence

Moments of Presence

Personal Essays

RICHARD W. WILBERG

CKBooks Publishing

Publisher's Cataloging-in-Publication Data
Names: Wilberg, Richard W., 1943-, author.
Title: Moments of presence : personal essays / Richard W. Wilberg.
Description: New Glarus, WI : CKBooks Publishing, 2025. |
Summary: In these sixty essays, the author helps readers discover our truth, build self-esteem, and choose what may not seem possible. The book reminds readers to be aware in this moment and search for personal meaning in life to create the way to our dreams.
Identifiers: LCCN 2025903878 | ISBN 9781966219033 (pbk.) | ISBN 9781966219040 (ebook)
Subjects: LCSH: Wilberg, Richard W.¬ –1943 - . | Coming of age. | Conduct of life. | Meaning (Philosophy). | Choice (Psychology). | LCGFT: Essays. | BISAC: BIOGRAPHY & AUTOBIOGRAPHY / Personal Memoirs. | LITERARY COLLECTIONS / Essays. | SELF-HELP / Motivational & Inspirational.
Classification: LCC CT275.W55.A5 2025 | DDC 920.71 W--dc23
LC record available at https://lccn.loc.gov/2025903878

CKBooks Publishing
PO Box 214
New Glarus, WI, 53574
ckbookspublishing.com

Images:
Richard W. Wilberg:
　　Front cover, The Lie · xiv, Seeking My Truth · 142
Family photo:
　　Before the Lie · 85
Walter Whalen:
　　Ping Pong with Dad · 105, Darts with Dad · 108
Wayne Brabender:
　　Back cover (author)

Songs:
Richard W. Wilberg:
　　Last Ride · 72-73, Search Until We Find · 114,
　　Meta · 174-175

Other:
Peggy Joque Williams · Editing
Christine Keleny · CKBooks Publishing

Contact or follow Richard at:
　　r_wilberg@yahoo.com
　　www.rwilberg.com/contact/
　　https://www.linkedin.com/feed/
　　www.x.com/@r_wilberg
　　https://richardwilberg.substack.com/
　　https://soundcloud.com/richard-wilberg-music/

Table of Contents

Part Three ~ Seeking My Truth

Preface

This book includes 60 essays described by a friend as "individual moments of presence that constitute a life." At the end of 2012, I retired from a forty-year career as a business leader, executive, and consultant. Origins of this book may be traced to this point.

Realizing that the primary responsibility of leaders is to develop ourselves and the people whom we lead, I launched a second career as a life and business coach. I obtained professional coach training at the University of Wisconsin-Madison. Ultimately, I received Professional Certified Coach (PCC) certification from the International Coaching Federation (ICF).

I began to blog. My first posts were self-help articles. As I coached and wrote, I discovered moments of presence in my life that could benefit others. With reflection, these situations became stories and ultimately essays. Magazines and journals published several of my stories and essays.

Why stories? Human cultures thrive and survive through examples of understood truths expressed in cultural beliefs. Stories have potential to educate and heal. We crave myths, legends, fables, and folklore because they are recognized as metaphors for truth, parables for understanding, and examples of how we may use cultural wisdom to live a meaningful life.

Stories began in oral tradition. Around our original ancestors' fire circles, mysteries of the universe were explained through words, music, dance, and play. Bards who traveled western civilization provided similar education and entertainment. Actors in these distant experiences were from the human, animal, plant, physical, and spiritual worlds.

For western culture, time is linear. First Peoples, however, believe past, present, and future coexist. When I look at actors in life's plays, I may witness history, but my vision is attuned to the present moment. Within the context of the present moment and non-linear time, essays in this book move forward and backward in time. Essays are written in first-person, present-tense except where past-tense better meets the needs of a particular essay.

Why essays? Essays are stories that focus on the author. See Phillip Lopate in *The Art of the Personal Essay* (1995) for further discussion. Essays in my book are based on my personal experiences. People, events, and dates are accurate, except where noted. Mr. Wagner, my grade school baseball coach, seventh grade teacher, and camera club leader, merits additional explanation. I've re-imagined him with extraordinary personal attributes. For the purpose of these essays, I've created a character who interacted with me more deeply and in a manner that suits my essays, rather than how he actually did. I portray Mr. Wagner as a mentor and a spiritual guide at critical times in my life. At these turning points, when I needed more than a baseball coach, the re-imagined Mr. Wagner appears and helps me move toward positive choice. I have also re-imagined two college professors (Dr. Reimer and Dr. Brundage) who taught me how to think. I respectively renamed them Dr. Livingston and Dr. Spencer.

There are no essays or stories about my wife, Suzan McVicker, in this book. Some names and locations have been changed to protect individuals. Sam Smith, his family, and Loon Lake Lodge represent an actual real estate transaction in Northern Wisconsin. Former owners requested anonymity. Names of coaching and mentoring clients have been changed to protect confidentiality.

Why this book now? We live in a time of constant change, deep fakes, eroding trust, rigid beliefs, and questionable truth. We seek solutions to our problems and may be nostalgic for the apparent simplicity of the past. Yet, all we have is now. If we are aware in this moment, today, and search for personal meaning in life, we may create the way to our dreams.

Within this context, in my eighth decade, I wrote this book to describe my journey. Through authorship, I've come to terms with a belief I've held most of my life. I thought I wasn't enough: big, strong, handsome, smart, you name it—the adolescent lie I told myself. People, animals, and the physical and spiritual worlds mentored, coached, and helped me build self-esteem to become whom I wanted to be. Through presence and creative choice, I changed my beliefs in life and career to continually seek my truth. Although this collection of reflections has been published, self-discovery continues. What's next? We'll see.

Introduction

How we create our lives and careers depends on our beliefs and the choices we make. Begin with the premise that we create the way to our future, consciously and unconsciously. If we choose to be a creative participant toward the future we want, yes, there may be obstacles to our plans. Some may be significant and derail our efforts. Others, however, such as self-limiting beliefs—like the lies we believe about ourselves—may be overcome if we adopt alternative ideas (reframe circumstances) and exercise our innate ability to choose what may not seem possible. When painted into a corner, for example, *move the corner.*

Presence expands choice. When we're present, we're alive in the moment. We're aware and possibilities bloom. We sense, emote, think, and feel about now, not yesterday or tomorrow. We set aside our *to do* list and focus on *being.* Cornelia Shipley, one of my coaching mentors, said to me, "Richard, who do you need to be to do what you want to *do?*" This question drives my personal life and coaching practice.

Being, rather than doing, is a core theme in this book. When we focus on being, we're present. When we're present, we embrace opportunity to react to what is real rather than imagined, assumed, or believed to be true. We'll validate our emotions, thoughts, and feelings against what's authentic and desirable for us (our individual truth). We'll ask, Is this right for me? and Is this what I desire?

Every day we make choices, profound and mundane, to propel us toward or away from our goals. Presence with ability to creatively visualize alternatives is most important. But I'm not a creative person, you might say. Welcome to the club of disbelievers. Give yourself permission to be creative. You are an innately creative individual.

"Does the river care about the boulder in his path?" a First People elder who requested anonymity asked me. "No, the river flows around the obstacle." Choice. Often you feel you have none. Being creative expands possibility. Possibility broadens choice.

Although moments of presence in this book are unique for me, you, dear reader, may have similar life experiences. Be aware and reflect on your moments of presence. Choose to move corners that block you. Become who you need to be to create the life you want.

PART ONE

The Lie

Auditorium Host

Some students at Nicolet High School in Glendale, Wisconsin, in autumn 1957 are known as auditorium hosts. They collect tickets, distribute programs, and escort classmates and guests to their seats. I'm fourteen, a freshman. At one special event I sit with my mom. A host walks past our aisle seat.

"Dick," she touches my arm. "Such nice boys and girls."

"No." I slump lower in my seat.

I am Dick, born at St. Joseph Hospital in Milwaukee, Wisconsin, in 1943. My father is Wesley Frank Wilberg, and Helen Grace Wilberg is my mother. Although my birth certificate names me Wesley Richard Wilberg, Mom calls me Dick.

"I don't ever want you to be junior," she responds to one of my childhood questions. "Your first name will always be Richard."

Okay, that seems simple enough, although throughout my life she calls me Dicky or Dick, but never Richard. My maternal Aunt Phyllis (who later changes her name to Ryann) nicknames me Dicky Bird and Sergeant Duck Eye. Maternal Uncle Wally's favorite names for me include Coots Man, Spider, and The Big Dumb Kid. My friends call me Dicky, Dick, and Richard until later in life when I insist that my name is Richard. And after I become known as Richard, new acquaintances ask if I go by Rich, Rick, and even Ricardo.

After a lifetime of various names, none of them legal, I have become Wesley once again. My 2025 Real ID, driver's license, and passport prove who I am, Wesley Richard Wilberg. Really? I'll be Richard for now.

∽

A week or so after sitting with Mom at Nicolet, I lie on my bed at our home in Fox Point, a Milwaukee suburb. I ponder my terse reply to her joy about auditorium hosts. Hosts are theater majors, part of a group of college-bound kids known as academics. I run with a group of friends who fix old automobiles. Hot rods, we call our cars. Hosts and academics call us greasers. School athletes, also known as jocks, make up the rest. Sometimes jocks join academics, never greasers.

Three divisions of students. Except for jocks, you belong to one. Never by choice, you accept your assignment. But here's the rub. I operate the movie projector at high school, and some kids see me as a host. Hey, I only run the projector and love movies. I'm not a host.

Dad owns a Keystone-brand 16mm movie projector. He films home movies and taught me how to run films for family entertainment. Since 8mm home-movie technology produces lower quality images, Dad uses the same state-of-the-art film format as Nicolet. I don't remember how I became the sole school projectionist. There are at least ten hosts. I'm not one of them. I'm above them.

Each time I show a movie, I climb carpeted steps to the projection room over the heads of my classmates. When I flip the switch to start a film, I stop all conversation and turn heads toward the screen. I get my classmate's attention.

Dad's Keystone projector runs movies on small reels of eight to ten minutes long. Known as shorts, these films include home movies, cartoons, and newsreels that cover one year or less. When I run more than one short at home, I have to change reels. Each swap requires that the lights be turned on and the next film threaded through the projector, a process that is prone to error. When I change reels, I destroy the mood of a darkened room, the feeling of escape inherent in viewing motion pictures.

I want to run feature films, movies that last for more than thirty minutes in a dark room. A projector that could accommodate larger, feature-length reels would meet my need. I want a movie projector like the 16mm Ampro Model 20 at high school.

Cast-iron constructed, of art-deco design with a textured, tawny-colored surface, Model 20 at Nicolet resembles a lion on four stump-like legs. An upright, cast-iron housing contains the projector's lamp, film drive mechanism, and lens. Vertical cooling fins drape from the housing like a lion's mane flowing from the head of an Egyptian sphinx. A metal plate attached to the projector bears the name *Ampro Precision Projector*.

Ampro stands at the edge of Nicolet's projection table and sends images across a valley of students to a movie screen at the opposite side of the auditorium. Years later I will see a poster of *The Lion King*. From the precipice of a rocky bluff, he roars to the crowd below him as if to say, "Look at me." I will remember Ampro, the lion of Nicolet.

Ampro's predecessor company, Universal Stamping and MFG Co., established in 1913, produced high-quality 16mm movie projectors. In 1926 the Chicago-based company broadened their line of silent film projectors to include sound to meet demand for new talkie films. Renamed Ampro Corporation in 1940, the company expanded production of their most popular product. Dominant in the WWII and early post-war period, Ampro in the mid-1950s faced competition from lower-priced projectors and television. Production ended in 1958.

On weekends, Dad and Mom take my sister and me to their favorite movie theater, the Egyptian. Located on Teutonia Avenue in northwest Milwaukee, the Egyptian runs feature-length films. In her confines, I experience the terror, mystery, and heartbreak of Hollywood's finest movies.

A palace of entertainment and intrigue, the Egyptian's lobby contains statues in the image of the god-kings of ancient Egypt, pharaohs who stand adjacent to simulated Roman columns. Passageways festooned with curtains, simulated flaming urns, and velvet drapes represent a Middle Eastern bazaar. When I turn in my seat while I watch a film, I look back at the projection room. I imagine a theater-sized Ampro, the lion of the Egyptian.

Movies will run at the Egyptian until she closes in the mid-1970s. Box-style, multi-plex cinemas in shopping malls will replace the Egyptian, and other glamorous stand-alone movie theaters. When demolished in 1984, the Egyptian will pass into memory like the pharaohs and flaming urns she emulated in her lobby.

⤴

One summer day, I slip into our living room and stand behind Dad as he reads the *Milwaukee Sentinel*, the morning newspaper.

"Dad. I want to buy a 16mm Ampro movie projector to show feature-length films."

"Dick, please sit beside me." He pats the sofa. "Have you earned enough money from your paper route to buy a new movie projector?"

"Sure." I join him on the sofa. "I have my savings in this oatmeal box." I place the container on the coffee table in front of us.

"Where could you buy—what do you call it—an Ampro?"

"At Blackhawk Films in Davenport," I say. "They sell movies and projectors. Uncle Wally drives to Iowa every month. He invited me to ride with him, and we can stop at Blackhawk. I've studied their catalog. They sell and service all brands of projectors. Blackhawk also has feature-length films to start my own collection."

"Good deal," Dad says. "I'm glad you'll get what you want."

Blackhawk Films, founded by Kent D. Eastin, opened in Davenport in 1932 to collect, restore, and preserve classic 35mm, 16mm, 8mm, and Super 8 motion picture films. Blackhawk mailed a catalog, in the style of a mimeographed newsletter, world-wide. I received their hand-crafted missives and spent hours lost in imagination. Over-the-counter sales in Davenport would end 1957. Ownership would change in 1975 to market films through Betamax, DVD, and later compact disk. Television would replace these formats. In 2020 Blackhawk's successor company would transfer their remaining film collection to preservationists in Paris, France, and keep an office in Burbank, California.

∾

Later that summer Uncle Wally wheels his Buick Roadmaster into our driveway early one morning to drive to Davenport. "Ready for our trip?"

"I'm really excited." I slide across the leather passenger seat already warmed by the sun. "Our visit to Blackhawk will be like a vacation in Hollywood."

"Great." Uncle Wally gently punches my arm. "I'm happy to help you with your plans. Let's hit the road!"

Road indeed. We leave Milwaukee on US Highway 18, also known as Bluemound Road, named for the village of Blue Mounds, Wisconsin, about a hundred miles west of Milwaukee. Constructed in 1926, US 18 begins in Milwaukee and ends 1,043 miles west in Orin, Wyoming.

Although heading to Davenport, Uncle Wally makes the first stop for his business in Madison, Wisconsin. He sells women's clothing to department stores. After Madison, US 18 becomes two lanes of winding asphalt pavement through a hilly portion of southwest Wisconsin known as the Driftless Area.

Untouched by the last glacier that retreated about twelve thousand years earlier, this portion of Wisconsin lacks glacial debris or drift. Instead, a pristine pre-glacial landscape of hills, valleys, bluffs, and winding rivers (a trout fishing paradise) survives for today's enjoyment. By 1989 the State of Wisconsin will have reconstructed US 18, described as "improvements." A four-lane ribbon of concrete pavement with limited access, designed to expressway standards, will replace the current two lanes. With curves eliminated, hills flattened, and bluffs truncated, US 18 will bypass Blue Mounds and other towns and businesses in favor of safety, speed, and convenience.

Today, however, after three slow hours through the Driftless Area, Uncle Wally's dashboard temperature gauge registers ninety-five degrees. We pull off the highway in Dodgeville, Wisconsin, for a business stop and to add water to the Buick's radiator. Uncle Wally chooses water instead of radiator fluid, deemed by some to be a better coolant. He tells a story about a household pet that died after drinking radiator fluid.

"Better isn't necessarily best," he says.

We leave Dodgeville on US 151, make another business stop in Dubuque, Iowa, and head south on US 60. After one more department store visit, we arrive in Davenport. He wheels the Roadmaster through a parking lot to stop at the front door of a single-story, metal warehouse building. A neon sign flickers Blackhawk Films.

"Hollywood, huh?" He laughs. "Let's go in."

A man sits behind a glass counter. He sports crew-cut hair and wears a denim work shirt. His name is stenciled above the right pocket. Maybe the name is Gus, Ben, or possibly Dan. I'm not certain. Let's assume his name is Gus. Behind him, movie boxes jam metal shelves.

"Welcome to Blackhawk Films." Gus bounces from his

chair; a newspaper falls on the floor. "What may I help you with?"

"My nephew, Dick, wants to buy a 16mm movie projector," Uncle Wally says.

"Howdy, Dick." Gus pumps my arm and points toward a table at the back of the store.

"I'm sorry but we don't have many. What brand are you after?"

"I want an Ampro Model 20." I shuffle my feet.

"We don't have any more Ampros," he says.

"Your catalog says you sell all makes and models." I look down at my shoes.

"Sold all of them. You should have come last week. I've got a nice Victor I'll sell you."

"RCA Victor?" I look at Gus.

"No, just plain Victor. Victor Model 60, actually. It's newer and better than an Ampro with arms for reels on the top. You can put this projector on a tabletop. You don't need a special stand like you do for an Ampro. Victor is convenient and easily stores in your closet."

"Never heard of Victor." I sigh.

"Look, Dick, do you want a movie projector or not?" Gus looks toward the back of the store. "Come on, I'll show you."

Victor Animatograph Corporation, an early manufacturer of motion picture equipment, began operations in Davenport. Affiliated with Blackhawk Films, Victor produced their first 16mm movie projector in 1923, the same year as Eastman Kodak.

Gus hefts a Victor Model 60 from a shelf onto a nearby table. As he said, top mounted reels fold into a compact, rectangular, utilitarian-designed, battleship-gray sheet-metal body. At table height, Model 60 with reels extended remind me of our family's television set with a rabbit ear antenna, no resemblance to the lion of Nicolet.

A half-hour later Uncle Wally loads the Victor into his trunk along with four cartoons and three newsreels that cover world events from 1942, 1943, and 1944. Gus didn't have any feature-length films. He must have sold them last week, too.

"Glad you stopped in." Gus stands in the store's doorway. "Come back again."

Uncle Wally nods to him and gives me a hug.

"Hey, Dick, too bad you didn't get what you wanted." He puts the Buick in gear, and we head for Milwaukee. "Maybe you'll have a good time anyway."

I love winter. No outside chores or paper route to distract me from my movies. By mid-January of the next year, I had borrowed enough folding chairs from family and neighbors to create a small movie theater in our basement. Dad places our home movie screen in front of the rows of chairs he had set out.

"You'll probably need all of these," he says.

I set the Victor on a folding table in the back of the room. Mom makes black curtains to cover the basement windows and hangs a velvet drape at the entrance to the basement. She decorates the post at the bottom of the stairs to look like a Roman column at the Egyptian.

"Isn't this great," she says.

Beside the column I place a flowerpot stuffed with red tissue paper—my flaming urn. I make flyers and tickets that announce a free movie every Saturday afternoon in February, and I distribute them at high school. I title the movie *World War II:1942 to 1944*. To create this feature film about the war years, I splice together the three newsreels purchased from Gus. Although I didn't have a film for each year of the war, I reason that 1942 through 1944 represents most of the war, the middle years. For every matinee I would add a cartoon before the movie so that each show would begin with a different cartoon, just like at the Egyptian.

An hour before the first show in February, my sister Lauren makes bowls of popcorn she places on a table at the bottom of the stairs. Dad sets bottles of soda pop beside the popcorn. Uncle Wally arrives early.

"Hey, Dick." He hands me a silver dollar. "I know the movie is free, but here's the first buck you'll earn doing what you love."

"Walter." Mom waves from the kitchen window. "Come in for coffee. And Dick, there's a line of kids by the basement door. Such nice boys and girls."

Dad was right. My premier will be a full house. I gesture to Lauren at the top of the stairs to begin collecting tickets and rush past the velvet drape. Down the stairs I fly and stand beside the Roman column. Before I start the movie, I greet each guest and escort them to their seat.

Bones

One late-winter day, possibly in 1958, I stand with a group of boys on a basketball court in Nicolet's gymnasium.

"Okay, guys, line up," Coach Johnson booms.

I shiver in my T-shirt and gym shorts. Mr. Johnson is a basketball coach and math teacher. I have him for both. He yells in math class, too.

"You—Chapman—at the head of the line, start the count by shouting one." Mr. Johnson jerks his thumb in Pete's direction. "Then Horton, you're two, and so on down the line. Even numbers will be shirts and will cover this goal. Odd numbers will be skins."

"Three, four, five…" the boys ahead of me shout.

I lean out of line and count heads to see if I will be even or odd. If I knew ahead of time, I could switch places in line with my friend, Jimmy. He knows I hate to be a skin and would gladly change places with me.

"Six, seven, eight…" the boys continue to count.

Darn, I'll be odd! There's not enough time to switch.

"Thirteen," my voice quivers. I peel off my T-shirt, the armor that cloaks the shame of my partially naked, pale-white body, and run to the far court. I stand six feet tall and weigh

130 pounds. The boys see my bony arms, rib bones, and chest so flat that I'm able to squeeze between our basement furnace and a column to retrieve an errant ping-pong ball. No wonder Uncle Wally calls me Spider.

"Okay, Sunshine," Coach Johnson bellows as he heaves a basketball at me with his .50-caliber-machine-gun arms. His cannonball flies between my BB-gun arms, slams into my chest, and knocks me to the floor.

What's wrong with me? I struggle to stand while he laughs.

"Let's pick it up, Sunshine." He sneers. "I've never seen such skinny arms. Let's put some meat on those bones."

Why does he have to call me Sunshine? That's not my name. I wish I could look and act like the muscle man on the beach in the *Charles Atlas* comic book ad who kicks sand in the face of a ninety-seven-pound weakling. If I were a real man, with a name like Rocco instead of Dick, I would punch Mr. Johnson in the face. I dribble toward the shirts. All my friends see who I am.

About two weeks later, I stand with a group of friends in Nicolet's auditorium lobby during intermission for the marching band's concert. I play sixth-chair trombone.

"Sergeant Duck Eye, stay right there!" Aunt Phyllis waves both arms over her head and surges through a crowd of students and parents toward me.

I crouch down in a futile attempt to escape. Too late. My friends laugh and disappear as Aunt Phyllis wraps her arms around me. She's Mom's youngest sister, not much older than me.

About a week later, Uncle Wally finds me alone in my bedroom. "Hey, Spider," he says. "May I come in?"

I nod and scoot over to make room on my bed. Spider is one of the few nicknames I tolerate.

"I heard about your Aunt Phyllis at the band concert," he says. "Embarrassing, huh?"

I shrug.

"Often, we don't like names we are called. Did you know the name on your Aunt Phyllis' birth certificate is 'Felix'? She ignores that mistake and goes by Phyllis. Don't let the name she calls you bother you. She loves you. Sometimes names really hurt, like my original family name. Did you know my name wasn't always Walter Whalen?"

"No, what was your name before?"

"Walter Smilnetsky. During the war, some soldiers in my platoon gave me a hard time about my Russian name. After the war ended, I received even more harassment. Your other aunts and uncles had similar experiences. So, we decided to change our name, but we couldn't agree on a new one. One day, most of us were seated on our front porch. Suddenly your Uncle John jumps up, points to a truck that passes by, and yells, 'That's it.' The name on the truck said: *Whalen Moving and Storage.* The next week we changed our name to Whalen."

Maybe fifty years after Uncle Wally's story, I squint into a Meade ETX-90 telescope eyepiece at the University of Wisconsin-Madison Astronomy Club star-gazing party in Cross

Plains, Wisconsin. Why is the best view of planets always on the coldest winter nights? Knowledge of the answer to my rhetorical question doesn't lessen the chill. The constellation Orion blazes overhead—jewels that float in a sea of black velvet.

"I still don't see the rings." My eyes water as I shiver.

"If you want to see Saturn's rings, avert your vision," the club leader says.

"Avert my vision, what do you mean?"

"Your eye includes rods and cones to collect light." Rods are located at the back of your eye, in the center, behind the pupil. Rods are sensitive to bright light for daytime vision. Cones surround the rods. Cones gather faint light from distant stars and planets. To use your cones, look to the side of your eye while you stare forward like when you have an eye exam. Remember how the doctor holds this hand to the right or left of your eye while you stare forward, and he asks, 'How many fingers?'"

"I see the rings," I shout. A fuzzy swirl swims in the eyepiece.

"If you want to see Saturn's rings, look past what's right in front of you."

Brown Socks

I stand beside schoolmate Jeannie in Nicolet's cafeteria in the spring of 1959. She mentions her friend Betty. I have a crush on Betty, although Butch is her boyfriend.

"Betty likes you, Dick." Jeannie blushes, flips her ponytail, and walks away.

"Wait." I reach for Jeannie's arm. "How do you know?"

"Everyone knows."

"Everyone but me." I chuckle. "Who told you?"

"Sue."

"Sue? How would Sue know? Betty is going steady with Butch. Why would she like me?"

"I don't know—I've got to go. Why don't you ask Betty? She'll be at the sock hop Saturday night."

A few days later, I show up at the dance. Vinyl-padded folding chairs line two sides of Nicolet's gym. Girls sit on the right under letters stenciled *Home* on concrete block walls. Boys sit on the left under similar letters that say *Visitors*. The scoreboard at the back of the gym shows the results from the earlier basketball game: *Home 54, Visitors 22.* I should be pleased with our team's victory, but tonight I feel like a visitor. I grab a chair next to Pete.

"Hey, Dick, how's it going?" he says.

"I'd rather be at home working on my hot rod," I say.

"Me, too. How's your progress on the coupe? Did you get the big-block Olds engine yet?"

"Nah." I slump in my chair. "I need a girlfriend first."

"Sit up, son." I imagine Mom's words. I look at my feet. Heavy brown socks bulge from below my pants. All the kids wear white socks and penny loafers. At sock hops they sport white socks without shoes, so I asked Mom for white socks.

"Perfect for a hop." She handed me a pair of Dad's brown socks. "Why don't you ask Cheryl or Shirley to the dance? They're such nice sisters."

"Ma," I stammer. "Cheryl and Shirley are twins. I'd have to pick one. How would the other feel?"

"Invite both," she says. "It's only a dance, not a date."

The band includes two students who play accordions, a drummer, and a lead singer, my friend Johnny. They strike up a waltz that sounds more like a polka in 2/4 time. I polka as well as waltz. Although I love fast-paced music, rock and roll especially, fast dances like the bop, jack, or jitterbug with a girl are a challenge.

Betty sits across the gym. Raven black hair shines in moonbeams of gym light, Aphrodite of Nicolet. Every guy wants her to be his gal. She talks to Sue, maybe about me?

Now's my chance to ask her to dance. She'll probably say no. What would she see in a shy boy like me?

Couples glide to the dance floor. I better get over to Betty. But it's ten miles across the dance floor and a thousand friends will watch me. What if she turns me down? What will the gang say on Monday? It's now or never. I snake through couples on the dance floor to arrive at the girl's side.

"Hi, Betty," I stammer. "Would you like to dance?"

"Ah, Dick. You're a real a sweet guy, but I won't dance with you. I'm going steady with Butch."

"Okay." I dip my head. "See you later, alligator."

She doesn't reply. I slosh back through the swamp of dancers. The waltz ends as I slump back into my chair.

"Did you dance with Betty?" Pete looks at me.

I shake my head.

"Probably your brown socks," he says. "I'll loan you a pair of white socks for the next dance."

"Okay, Rockers, enough of your father's music," Johnny shouts into the mic. "How about some rock and roll? Ready to bop to Chuck Berry?"

Pete stands. I follow him with a group of boys to the dance floor. Girls flood to the floor in unison. Everyone dances alone.

Maybe a week later, Dad installs a three-inch diameter, white-painted metal screw-jack pole between the concrete basement floor in our home and the exposed first floor joists at the foot of our basement stairs. "Sagging stairs," he says.

"My girlfriend," I reply.

Dad scratches his head as I run to the phone to call Pete. "Come on over," I say. "We'll practice the bop."

And we did. Every afternoon after school, we'd rush to my basement. I'd grab the pole, as if it were Betty's hand, first with my right hand, then with my left, and lean back. I'd bop to Elvis as he crooned "Heartbreak Hotel" from my Emerson 45 rpm portable phonograph. Then Pete would take his turn. We alternated and danced until he would leave for dinner. The pole never declined our invitations to dance.

Two or three weeks later, at the last sock hop before summer vacation, I stride across the dance floor to the boy's side of the gym, sporting a pair of Pete's white socks.

"Hey, Pete, how's it going?" I slump in my familiar folding chair and immediately correct my posture.

"Not bad." Pete looks at my feet. "Nice socks."

I see Jeannie nod to Sue. She's probably talking about Betty. Except, Jeannie looks across the gym at me. For an instant, our eyes meet. My heart races. How come I've never noticed Jeannie before? Johnny strikes up "Why Do Fools Fall In Love?" I bop across the dance floor, Pete in my shadow.

"Jeannie, would you like to dance?" My voice is firm.

"I thought you'd never ask, Dick." Jeannie takes my hand. She swings on my right hand, then my left and leans back. "You really can dance."

Lie to Me

One day in late spring, possibly 1959, I drive Jeannie home from school. We pass a 1956 Pontiac four-door sedan parked in the shade on the west-bound side of Fairy Chasm Road, in River Hills, Wisconsin, about a ten-minute drive from Nicolet. A cigarette glows, the only indication that the driver sits behind the wheel.

"Every day Carl waits on the hill and watches me come home from school." Jeannie touches my hand resting on the seat between us. "He was expelled from Nicolet. He carries a knife. My parents won't let me date him. That's okay. He scares me. Please drive the other way home after you drop me off. Okay, Dick?"

"I'm not afraid of him," I say. It's out of my way to drive west." My left hand tightens on the steering wheel. Jeannie releases my right hand.

"Please!" She kisses my cheek and leaves a smear of lipstick. "I don't want anything to happen. Drive west. I'll see you tomorrow."

My heart pounds as I back slowly out of Jeannie's driveway. *Thud, thud, thud.* My hot rod Oldsmobile 348 engine echoes my heart. I'll call Carl's bluff. What could happen? I'm not a wimp. I turn east and inch up the hill.

I'm ten feet from his car when the driver's door flies open. He struts to the centerline, a hulk of a boy in bib overalls, no shirt, and black leather scuffed boots. Carl's right muscular arm is raised like a traffic cop to halt my progress. I roll down my window. There's a bulge in his right pants pocket. Does he carry his knife? How long is the blade?

"Are you Dick?" He sneers.

"Yeah," I grunt.

"Stay away from her." His arm strikes through the open window like an uncoiled snake. He grabs my shirt.

"Okay, I will." I twist to dislodge his hand.

"I'll remember you." He releases his grip, presses his knuckles into my chin, and saunters back to his car.

A week later, I drive Jeannie home. To avoid Carl, I take the western route. Maybe he didn't see me, or I called his bluff? Would he pay me back next time I dropped her off? For the next weeks and months, I continue my alternate route. Still, he's always there. He waits, a sentinel in a watchtower, perched on the hill, always a threat of retaliation. And me in my car in a dance to avoid Carl, an impasse, a result of my lie.

Twenty or more years later and approximately seven thousand miles from River Hills in Dubai, UAE, I'm escorted into Amour Architects' conference room. Amour is my employer's Middle Eastern business partner. It's early September and summer's heat hasn't dissipated. A box of mahogany or another rare tropical wood, glossy finished with gilded corners and latches, sits on a polished conference table in the center of the room. The length of a yardstick and the width of a twelve-inch ruler, like the size my first grade teacher used to rap my knuckles, the majesty of the box captures my attention.

"Welcome to Dubai." Amour extends his hand. A gold cufflink pierces a French cuff that extends beyond his tailored suit sleeve. With the effects of jet lag still present, I almost fail to notice his impeccably groomed hair and handcrafted Italian shoes. Milan perhaps?

"Richard, Richard Wilberg, that is." I extend my hand. "I'm happy to meet you."

"Please join me at the conference table." Amour greets my colleagues in a similar gracious manner. "I have Arabian coffee and bottled water for refreshment. We'll talk, and then you'll be my guests for dinner. How was your trip from Chicago?"

"Uneventful," I say, "the way international travel should be. We left Friday night, stayed in Frankfort Saturday, and caught a flight to Dubai this morning. It's a long trip but we're ready for work."

"Good." Our host smiles. "The Sheikh is eager to see your feasibility study for the new office building."

"Thank you." I nod. "We are excited to review your design. But first, if I may—"

Amour nods.

"What's in the box?" I rub my chin. He slides the box across the table, opens the clasps, and lifts the lid. Fire from the setting sun reflects off the box. A scimitar rests on a velvet pillow.

"The handle is 24-carat gold with embedded rubies and emeralds," he says. "The finest German steel is used for the blade. This saber is my gift for our client. Tomorrow, before you present your feasibility study and I show my design for the office building, I will offer my gift."

"Beautiful. Please tell me more." I sip my coffee.

"In my country…" Amour nods. "Architects follow a custom to gift their clients a blade of superior quality, similar to our work. I will ask him to sever our relationship if he is not completely satisfied. Of course, I hope he will approve or, if he doesn't, that he will lie to me."

Lone Wolf

"*H*e is my hero." I thread 16mm black-and-white movie film around sprockets and behind the lens of my Victor movie projector. Jeannie and I stand in my basement, just prior to school break in the summer of 1959.

"Who is?" Jeannie lifts a cardboard box. "This Castle Films label says Hopalong Cassidy in *Lone Wolf*. Is Hoppy your hero?"

"Nah." I turn toward the basement wall switch to flip off the lights. "I like Lone Wolf. He's cool. He rides the range and doesn't have anyone to tell him what to do. He's a real man and—"

"Wait." Jeannie touches my elbow. "I'm confused. You like the bad guy and not the star of the movie?"

"Well, I like Hoppy, too," I say. "But I really like Lone Wolf." We sit side by side on foldable chairs in front of Dad's portable movie screen. "You'll see in the movie how cool he is. He sleeps in a tent and lives alone. He doesn't have chores around a house or live with a bossy family."

"Don't you like me, Dick?"

"Sure, I like you, Jeannie. You're my girlfriend."

"You have a reputation at school of being a loner. How

will you have a girlfriend or family in the future if you want to live alone?"

"I don't know." I reach for two bottles of Coke on a side table. "Why do I have to decide? I want both."

⌒

A few months later, Uncle Wally and I drive along a deserted country road. We had fished all day at Beaver Lake, about a forty-five-minute drive from home.

"Skunks!" I grab his arm. "Two of them."

"Where, Dick?"

"On the edge of the road to the right of the headlights—"

"I see them." Uncle Wally slows the car and leans forward for a better view.

"They don't seem to be in a rush to get away." I roll down my window. "In fact, they may have slowed their pace to a saunter since they first appeared in our headlights."

"A skunk's vision is limited." Uncle Wally pulls to the side of the road to watch striped tails merge with tall grass. "Skunk can't see what approaches him. Also, what seems to be his lack of awareness gives us a false impression that he isn't concerned about us. His act of indifference gives a skunk the reputation of being a loner. Quite the contrary is true. A skunk is a social animal. He just wants to be seen."

"Why?"

"A skunk doesn't want a confrontation. Most wild animals run or aggressively stand ground when humans approach. Not skunk. His first line of defense is to be seen and then to disappear. A skunk's second line of defense is his spray. He avoids spray because his response is limited. Once spray is dissipated, a skunk is completely defenseless."

"Come to think of it, I've usually seen skunks at a distance," I say.

"He doesn't want you or his predators to mistake him for a rabbit or some other easy prey. So instead of rapid escape, a skunk slowly walks away. He doesn't want to be alone. He just wants to be left alone."

Whistle Again

One afternoon when sixteen or seventeen, I sit in our living room with my friend, Davy.

"Why would your dad give you, his Studebaker?" Davy leans back in the armchair across from me. He and I share a common interest in automobiles, so I'm not surprised by his question.

"Is the car, okay?"

"She's okay…sort of," I say. "Last week Dad parked the Green Hornet, as he calls her, in front of the house. I'm outside to mow the lawn. A guy pulls around the corner too fast and bam, like boxcars in a freight train that slam together he sideswipes the driver's side of the Hornet. He gets out, shrugs his shoulders, and waves to Dad who watches from inside the house. Dad waves back. The man jumps into his car and speeds away. Either Dad didn't hear the crash and assumed there was no damage, or he didn't want a confrontation."

"Wow, what did you do next?" Davy shakes his head.

"I'm curious why Dad let the guy go, so I run into the house to tell him about the damage, and he gives me his car."

"What are you going to do with her since the driver's

door is caved in? Looks like you can't open the door or roll down the window."

"I don't know. I liked her the way she was before the crash. Maybe I'll junk her and use the coins to buy some Blatz beers for you and me at Marty Zivkos."

"Why don't we make the Green Hornet into a convertible?" Davy chimes. "You always wanted a rag-top but couldn't afford one. My uncle has an electric saber saw. If we cut off the roof you won't need the door. You could jump in and out just like those cool surfers do with their hot rod T-buckets."

"Are you crazy?" I spring from my chair and wave my arms. "We live in Milwaukee, not Malibu. Convertibles don't have four doors, and they have a fold-away roof. After we saw off the roof, how'll we finish the jagged metal and make a collapsible roof? Besides that, how will we pick up girls with the driver's door caved in? No one will want to ride with us."

"Easy," Davy croons. "We'll cover the rough metal with black electrical tape. When we cruise Wisconsin Avenue to look for girls, they walk on the sidewalk, right? They'll never see the left side of the Hornet. I'll let them into the back seat from the right side. Girls want to ride in a convertible on a hot summer night. They won't notice the tape in the dark, only two cool high school guys in a convertible. And you don't need a roof on your car. When was the last time you bombed the avenue in rain or winter? Never. Think about how great a convertible will be and how many dates we'll get."

"Ah, I don't know," I say. "I've never done anything like this before."

∽

Over fifty years later, Davy and I sit in his living room in Bayside, Wisconsin, about a five-minute drive from my former home in Fox Point. He has lived in the same house since high school. He whistles while he smokes, always did. Few things change for Davy. Suppose we had this conversation:

"Whistle that tune again," I say. "I really like that tune."

"Impossible, Richard." He leans back in his chair. "The melody is gone."

Life has been harder for Davy than me. After high school he enlisted to avoid the draft. He went to 'Nam anyway. Me, I received a student deferment and enrolled at the University of Wisconsin-Milwaukee. I planned to enlist or be drafted after graduation. The draft missed me, so I didn't have to decide.

"What do you mean gone?" My gut wrenches. "You whistled a haunting tune that sticks with me. Remember the music score in *The High and the Mighty*? I want a melody like that. Whistle again, just like before, and I'll get a recording on my phone. Your melody will be an important part of my song."

Davy's fingers, stained yellow from years of cigarettes and scarred from work at the brass mill, fiddle with his cigarette butt. He became a two-pack-a-day guy in the Army, always Camels. I gave up cigs in college—sort of. While Davy slogged through waist-high water in Vietnam, I marched in anti-war campus protests—sort of. Davy and I never talk about those days.

"Will it, Richard?" Davy looks up at me now. His eyes tell a story that words fail to explain. "Why does my whistle have to be just the way you want? Why isn't whatever melody I create good enough for you? I improvise. What I whistled is gone. Everything we have ever done is gone. I'll whistle another tune. What you'll hear will be different. If you're able to accept what I offer, I think you'll be pleased."

He lights another Camel. Dense, acrid smoke blocks my vision like the years between us block my understanding. We sit silently before the smoke lifts and his eyes meet mine.

"Remember when I wanted to cut the roof off the Green Hornet?" Davy frowns.

"Of course, I do. I thought your idea wouldn't work. Every time you came up with a solution to a problem, I found reasons why your plans would fail. You finally convinced me, and we made a convertible, not perfect, but okay."

"Now you tell me." He laughs. "All this time."

"You know what?" My heart races as I open a window. The air clears and I feel a fresh breeze. I turn to Davy.

"You're right." I smile. I want to talk about the Green Hornet, Davy's time in 'Nam, the distance between us, and all the conversations we never had. Instead, I say, "I'll get my phone. What you do will be good enough. Go ahead, whistle again."

Brass Knuckles

*D*avy and I sit on the patio at my home maybe in late summer 1959. "I need brass knuckles and probably a blackjack," I say as I reach for his pack of Camels on the heavily pockmarked cedar picnic table. We had turned the table on end the summer before to use it for bow and arrow target practice. Dad saw the holes and shrugged. Mom advised me to think before I did something foolish like that again.

"Brass knuckles?" Davy blows an oval smoke ring into the still air. "What the hell for?"

"For John VA." I light my smoke.

"Who the hell is John VA?" Davy exhales from his mouth and re-inhales lingering vapors through his nose.

"John Van Allan." I take a deep drag and cough. "Some guy who messes around with Jeannie. I want to scare him off just like Carl chased me away from Jeannie."

"That worked really well for Carl, as I remember." Davy laughs.

"Never mind that. Where could I get brass knuckles?"

"I don't know. Maybe we could go to Sears? You could ask the salesman. 'Excuse me, could you direct me to the brass knuckles department? I'd like to look at blackjacks, too.'

The salesman would probably say, 'Right this way young man. Do you need small, medium, or large?'"

"Could you be serious?" I shake my head. "I also need to practice how to fight. I found an article in one of Uncle Wally's *Argosy* magazines on how to have a fist fight. The article said to stand sideways to be a smaller target for my opponent. But how do I hit John if I stand sideways? One of my arms won't be long enough. I really don't want to fight him anyway, but I have no choice."

"Actually, you have many choices, Dick, but let's figure out how to make brass knuckles first. A blackjack will be easy. We'll pour buckshot into an old sock."

"Dad has lots of old brown socks."

"To make brass knuckles will be harder." Davy flicks an ash from his cigarette into his pant's cuff. "Maybe we could screw two carriage bolts together and wrap black electrical tape over the whole thing. Carriage bolts would be perfect because they have rounded ends that will be easier on your fingers when you slug John."

"That's not exactly brass knuckles. What about the nut holding the two bolts together?" I snuff out my half-finished smoke under my shoe. "When I hit John, won't the nut break my middle finger?"

"Well, don't hit him. Just show him your super brass knuckles and wicked blackjack, and he'll run away. Where do you plan to confront him?"

"Jeannie has a date with him next Friday night. I'll hide in the bushes in her front yard. When he brings her home and walks back to his car, I'll jump him."

"Cool." Davy takes his last drag and snuffs out the cig

with his finger and thumb. He puts the extinguished butt in his pant's cuff. "Sounds like a plan."

◦≈

The next Friday night I wait behind Jeannie's bushes. She's late. Man, it's cold. Branches scratch my ribs. Maybe I should go home? Wait—I see someone—it's him.

"Good night, John." Jeannie leans against her screen door.

"Good night, Kitten." John bends forward and kisses Jeannie on her cheek. Kitten! Blood pounds in my neck. I move branches for a better view as John walks along the path toward me.

"Hey, big man." I step from my shelter, hands in my pockets.

"Who's there?" He stops. "Are you Dick?"

"Yeah." I step forward. "What's it to you?" My shoulders shake.

"Jeannie talks a lot about you." He moves toward me. "I hoped I would get a chance to meet you."

"John?" Jeannie approaches from behind. "I didn't see your car leave. I was worried. Who's with you?"

"Dick." John faces Jeannie.

"Dick?" Jeannie turns toward me. "Why are you here? Why are your hands in your pockets? You're shaking. Are you cold?"

"No, I'm okay." I pull my hands from my pockets. "John and I were talking."

"What's that bulge in your pocket?" Jeannie walks toward me.

"Nothing." I shift from one leg to the other.

"I'm glad all three of us are here." Jeannie faces John and me. "John, why don't you tell Dick your news?"

"Well, okay." John shuffles his feet. "Next week my family will move to Texas. I'll leave Nicolet and finish high school in Austin."

Winner's Club

Strings screech, hum, and sing with a never-intended song. Honey and black-varnished maple, like the color of dappled afternoon sunlight absent from our windowless garage attic, breaks over Dad's knee. Splinters, like dead autumn leaves, fall to the attic floor. I'm 17 on this spring day in 1960.

"No one will ever play this again." Dad holds the wreckage of a mandolin aloft, as a victorious hunter lifts his kill. Dust, the stuff of creation, coats his hands and pants. "You need music lessons to play this. Who has time for that? Here, Dick, toss this junk in the trash."

"Dad, why did you wreck Mother's mandolin?" Memories of sweet music battle with tears. My feet stick with glue of uncertainty to the tongue-in-grove, brown-stained pine floor as I try to move toward this giant of a man who could destroy in an instant.

"Listen, son," he says. Light, from a naked 60-watt bulb hanging from red pine rafters, drapes Dad's ten-foot shadow over me. "A man I don't like gave the mandolin to her. You're too young to understand, but old enough to know what a man has to do. He must show he's boss. Real men are winners. Wimps are losers. Who do you want to be?"

"A man, I guess." The weight of his question holds me rigid.

"What's that?" Dad booms.

"A real man." My feet break free from indecision. Real men don't cry. I step toward him.

"I want to be a winner like you, Dad."

A month or so later, I tentatively step into the living room.

"Dad." My voice trembles.

"Yes, Dick."

"Could I go deer hunting with Davy and his pals over Thanksgiving weekend? I've never been to deer camp. Do you have a rifle I could use?"

"Come to the garage with me." He lays the *Milwaukee Sentinel* on the coffee table and lifts from his lounge chair. We climb a creaky wood stepladder to stand on familiar, brown-stained pine boards in the attic.

"Take this gun." He pushes a hex-barrel rifle with a honey-varnished walnut stock toward me. "This is a Model 1892 lever action, .25-20 caliber Winchester. It's not exactly a deer rifle. The bore is a bit small, more of a varmint gun, but it'll do. Some goofball tried to hammer his initials into the gun metal." Dad shakes his head. "Bullets go in here." He points to the magazine. "Although loaded, the gun is not armed until you cock the lever to place a round in the chamber. Release the safety and pull the trigger to shoot."

"Do I need lessons on safety?" The rifle is heavy with a weight of responsibility I will soon understand.

"Nah, I told you all you need to know."

❧

Later that year I bounce along Forest Road 73, two tire ruts that run through endless white pines near Mercer, Wisconsin. I ride in the open bed of Davy's Ford pickup. Dad's Winchester rests on my lap. Today is opening day for deer hunting.

Morning sun peeks through frosted boughs, crystals of brilliance in frigid air. Last night's snow dusted the woods. Davy's brother Tommy rides shotgun next to him. Pete, John, and Tom T. sit beside me along with essentials for deer camp. I remember last evening's *Outdoor Wisconsin* television show about the dangers of riding in pickups with a loaded rifle. I snap the safety on. Nervous energy flows as I finger the gun's disfiguring *HK* initials, an imperfect blunder. Who was HK? Was he a real man? Did HK wonder if he would kill? We lurch out of ruts and stop at the bottom of a valley. Davy leaps from the cab.

"Everyone out," he shouts. "We'll pitch camp after we hunt."

"Okay guys," Tommy yells with the volume of a drill sergeant. "Line up behind Davy. I'll hunt with him. Dick you're next, then Tom T. Pete and John will bring up the rear."

"Hey, Tommy, how will we hunt?" I fidget.

"We'll drop off each pair as we hike. One of you will sweep the woods to drive a buck into the open. Your partner will wait in the clearing and have first shot. We'll keep a half mile between pairs to minimize injury from stray bullets."

I laugh and stomp my cold feet. Could a stray bullet kill? Or would it fall from the sky like a harmless acorn that bounces off my head?

"Pay attention guys," Tommy continues. "Coach Lombardi says winning isn't everything, it's the only thing. Whoever bags the first buck will be the winner of this year's deer camp."

I lever a bullet into firing position, check the safety, and follow Tom T. My Winchester points away from him. Prairie grass changes to brush that grabs my arms and pulls the rifle toward him.

"Buck," Davy whispers. "Fan out."

Tom T. moves right. I follow and snap the Winchester's safety off. Twigs like woody fingers pull my hand. *Bang!* The varmint gun kicks upward. My bullet snaps a branch over Tom T.'s shoulder.

"What the hell!" He turns. "Are you trying to kill me?"

A month or so later, I walk to the front of the classroom at Nicolet. My homeroom teacher sits before me.

"Mr. Spooner, I'd like a hallway pass to visit the music department."

"Dick, to leave homeroom to visit the music department is unusual." He grades papers and turns from me to look over rows of desks, a sea of kids that crowd the room. "But you're a good student, so here's your pass."

I walk to the lower level. Paper turkeys, pilgrims, and pumpkins that adorned last week's corridors have been replaced with wintry holiday decorations. Silver stars and cotton puffs intended as snow promise change. Music Department in gold letters on the glass door indicates my arrival. I knock.

"Come in," a vigorous voice says. Mr. Bartz scans my pass and rubs his white goatee. "How may I help you, Dick?"

"I want to take mandolin lessons."

Move the Corner

"*J*ump in the hole, Wilberg." The foreman, whom I'll call Jones, kicks topsoil into an excavated pit beneath a house in the North 16th Street neighborhood in Milwaukee in early summer, 1961.

"Why, boss?" I stammer.

"We have to pull this painted lady out of the hole and get her across Clybourn Street before dawn." He pulls off his engineer's cap. *Schuette Movers* is barely readable through oil stains and grime. "Take this hammer and shims. Your job, on the rear corner of the house, is to fill gaps between the top of the wheel carriage, we call them dollies, and the 10-by-10 beams that carry this baby. Here, come on, I'll show you."

We scramble into the pit. My flashlight, though a cone of brilliance in Northern Wisconsin, is a mere candle beneath the home. Darkness infused with plaster dust and dirt filters my light. An eternity of cobwebs hanging from the basement ceiling caress my face like unwanted fingers. To find my station at the left rear corner of the house, I touch overhead joists for guidance, as a miner might feel his way through a cave. Foreman Jones joins me.

"Why are we moving this house, boss?" I shine my flashlight in a broad circle.

"Freeway will come through this block." He removes a work glove from his right hand and rubs his chin. "Since we won't reroute a freeway to save a beautiful Victorian home, this house was scheduled for demolition. Then someone hired us to move this painted lady."

"Why do you call her a painted lady, boss?"

"You ask a lot of questions. Let's see. I think the term has to do with how the architectural style broke from the past in the last part of the nineteenth century to reflect the wealth of the Victorian and Edwardian era. After World War II, many of these homes were renovated and repainted to follow California trends toward three or more colors. First day on the job?"

"Yup." I sneeze. "Excuse me. I just finished high school. I wanted a job instead of college. Dad called Mr. Schuette to get me this job."

"I thought so." He lights a cigarette, inhales deeply, and coughs. "Tough to smoke in all this dust. I better show you a thing or two. Store your shims above this 10-by-10." Jones points upward. "See how snug the wheel carriage fits against the timber? No gaps, right? As we pull her up the ramp, out of the hole, over the curb, and onto the street, gaps may open above the wheel carriage. If they do, use your hammer to pound shims into the gap to close the opening. Be careful of the wheels. Always work from behind the dolly. We don't want any accidents. I already had pancakes for breakfast, if you catch my drift."

"Sure." I laugh.

"Got to get back and check the rest of the crew." He

snuffs out his cig and replaces his cap. "Listen for the horn. Two short beeps will tell you we've started to pull. When we're out of the hole and onto the street, we'll stop, and you'll scoot out from under the house. Remember, your job is to move this corner. Six dollies support this house. I've got a man on each of the other five dollies. This corner is yours."

His flashlight beam swings side to side like a snake that slithers away from me. I move behind the wheels. Disconnected electric wires dangle from above and tickle my neck. I jump and bump my head as I grab hammer and shims. *Beep! Beep!* from beyond darkness. Beauty above me trembles and groans as she inches forward. Water drips from disconnected pipes to soak my shirt. I shiver. Painted lady moves as wheels crunch fallen plaster. I watch my feet and bang my elbow. The house raises like a Phoenix, after years of rest. I decide to enroll in college.

About seven-months later, I walk through the living room in a basement unit apartment on Farwell Avenue, a few blocks south of the University of Wisconsin-Milwaukee.

"Hi, I'm Richard." I greet a man who sits at a lunchroom-style table. "May I join you?" I juggle a pitcher of beer that overflows, a shot full spills on the table.

"Careful man, that's good stuff." He offers his hand, sticky from beer. "Clint here. Good to meet you, Richard."

"Pour you a beer?" I wipe my hand on my pants and lift the pitcher. Clint nods. I pour.

"Hey man, I want my beer in a cup not all over the table."

He stands and uses his right hand like a squeegee to guide spilled beer from the tabletop into his paper cup.

"Sorry, I didn't see your cup was upside down." I set the pitcher back on the table. "It's dark in here."

"My cup is always upside down when its empty." He wipes his wet hand on his shirt.

"That's how brothers know when we need another brew. Maybe you've had enough beer? Could I get you a glass of water?"

"Thanks. I need some water. Why does the sign at the door say the cover charge is for a new sofa?"

"We have to report our budget to the University." Clint leans closer. "Students Club is a college-sponsored activity. We're not permitted to take a collection for beer, so we say the money is for a new sofa. Are you new to the club?"

"Yes, my buddy Pete introduced me. He's in class right now, so I came alone to drown my sorrows."

"How so?"

"I got kicked out of college last month. I'm on probation."

"Yeah?" Clint grins. "I'm on probation, too."

"What for?" I raise my cup for a sip of water.

"Assault."

"Oh, no!" I gulp and spill water across the table.

"There you go again." He laughs.

"No, no! I'm on probation for bad grades."

Maybe two or three months later, I stand beneath a car hoisted on a grease rack at Red's Super Service on North Port Washington Road, about a mile or two up the road from Nicolet. I replace the car's oil drain plug. My wrench slips and I smash my knuckles into the engine pan. Snow and road-melt water dislodge from the fender. A salty bine drips into my eyes. I wipe my face and walk to the boss's office.

"Red, may I talk with you?" I lean through a white metal door covered with oily handprints. He scribbles a note on a pad of paper on top of a desk littered with ledgers, invoices, and other documents necessary to own and operate a gas station and repair garage. A Craftsman tool calendar hangs on a nail hammered into the wall. Chilton auto repair manuals line the shelf behind his desk.

"What do you want, Richard?" He continues to write and shuffle papers, eyes focused on his work. "I'm busy."

"May I come in?" I move toward an armchair that faces his desk. Cigarette butts overflow a bronze ashtray that stands next to the chair. "May I smoke?"

He looks up from his work, nods, and folds grease-smudged arms across his chest. A white oval patch with a red flying horse, a Pegasus, the emblem of Mobil Oil Corporation, is sewn to his work shirt.

"I've been here almost a year." I take a deep drag on my Lucky Strike and turn my head to blow smoke out the door. "I went to full time in January when I got kicked out of school. I like the work here, but I want more in life. I've decided to go back to college to get a degree. I'll leave at the end of August."

"August?" Red uncrosses his arms and leans back in his chair. He lights a Camel and blows smoke in my face. "You're kidding me. You won't quit in August. You're fired right now, college-boy. I never liked you anyway. I guess work as a grease monkey isn't good enough for you."

⌒◡

About thirty years later, I work at a company I'll call Robert & Sons Construction in Alsip, Illinois. My boss is vice president of industrial construction. He leans over the top of my modular-designed furniture cubicle. Our conversation goes something like this:

"Sell anything for me today, Richard?"

"Nothing today, Mark." I hang up my telephone, careful to keep the cord free of the shoulder brace attached to the receiver. "I make cold calls every morning."

"Ah—let's walk to my office to talk," he says.

I follow him through narrow corridors that connect several construction trailers twisted haphazardly in single file like a partially coiled snake. Each private office is decorated with a plastic, potted, palm tree. We arrive at a single-story red brick building that houses his office.

"Take a seat, Richard." Mark motions toward a vinyl-covered armchair opposite his desk. He wears a cap and work shirt. *Robert & Sons* is monogrammed above his right pocket. Mark swings his chair to the right, leans back, and props his work boot on a waste basket. Mud that clings to his boot dislodges, misses the container, and drops to the floor. "Nothing today, Richard? Is that right?"

"Yes." I look at a chunk of mud that remains on his boot. "Construction sales are not like boot sales. Boots, for example, may be sold as a commodity. You and I don't want to sell construction as a commodity. I need to build a relationship with each customer before they will contract with us to build a new building. Before you hired me, I spent three years with my prior employer selling $40 million worth of new office building construction. All contracts were negotiated sales without bids. We could bid construction work and, like a commodity, the lowest bidder would get the job. In bid construction, profit margins are low and risks are high—"

"Yes, I know all that." He lifts his boot from the basket, turns his chair, and faces me.

"But why does it take so long to make a deal? I hired you to find work in the industrial market. You've been here six months and no sales."

"I can't rush a client's decision." I lean forward toward Mark's desk. My hands grip the chair's arms. "I thought we agreed I would focus on the largest companies, those with the best potential for multiple construction projects. Larger businesses might not have a project immediately, but they could have many buildings in the future. I want to build relationships."

"True, but we need sales." He looks past me at a wall clock. "I'd offer you coffee but the machine is broken. How about some water?" He motions toward a pitcher on a side table. "Help yourself."

I pour myself a cup of water and return to my chair. "I could shift my focus to clients with an immediate need, but those customers might have less possibility for future work. I focus on companies with the best long-term potential for repeat business."

"It's time for your six-month review." He reaches in his desk drawer, removes a letter-sized sheet of paper, reviews the contents, and pushes it across the desk to me. "Read this."

My hand shakes as I hold a document titled, "Employee Evaluation." The form lists several open-ended questions, to which Mark has scrawled pencil-written answers. I notice erasure smudges, over written comments, and a line of five boxes at the bottom of the form. Boxes are labeled from left to right, "Excellent, Good, Average, Poor," and "Unsatisfactory." I look up from the form at Mark.

"I see you've put three x's over the box for 'Unsatisfactory.'" My hand is steady. "The form is designed for only one checkmark per box. You've either incorrectly filled out the form or do you say my work is triple unsatisfactory?"

He stares at me. His jaw drops open.

"Looks like you intend to fire me." I stand. "I saw this in the works so last week I talked to Robert—"

"Robert!" Mark stands. "You've got a lot of nerve to talk to the president of our company behind my back."

"Perhaps. But I don't see a future for me in industrial sales or in work for you." I pick up my cup of water and walk across the room to Mark's potted palm. "Robert said I could transfer to commercial sales at any time. I'll work directly for him. I'll accept his offer today." I pour water on the palm's plastic soil and leave the room.

Fly Out of Here

I sit in a lecture hall at the University of Wisconsin-Milwaukee. My professor, whom I'll call Dr. Livingston, walks to the front of the room. I imagine this conversation:

"Hello, students. I'm Professor Livingston. If you signed up for Biology 101, then this fine September morning is your first day of class. If so, you're in the right place. If not, please leave now."

A chuckle rolls through the room.

"Ha—you wonder, who is this character?" He grabs the lectern and peers over the top of his bifocals. "You probably also might ask yourself, if I'm Dr. Livingston, then where is the famous explorer and journalist, Henry Stanley? Unfortunately, Mr. Stanley and my esteemed namesake Dr. Livingston, missionary, explorer and no relation to me, died many years before you were born."

Student chuckles turn to laughter. He raises his hand and the audience goes silent. He has our attention. Learning is fun!

"Although I won't entertain you with jungle stories from the African Congo, I will challenge you to think differently." He scans the lecture hall.

"Mr. Wilberg, in the front row." He nods to me. "Yes, you. Why do insects have wings?"

"To fly," I say.

"Partially correct," Dr. Livingston continues. "Insects indeed use wings to fly. Mr. Wilberg; are there other reasons for insect wings?"

The lecture hall chair holds me captive like a bug's pincers hold its prey. Next time I won't sit in the front row. "To escape death?"

My classmates chuckle.

"Maybe." Professor Livingston's eyes swoop to meet mine. "Prior to wings, insects developed structures similar to radiator fins to dissipate body heat in the hot climate of the Carboniferous Period, 360 to 286 million years ago." He flaps his arms as if to fly. "Over time these fins expanded. Then with natural selection and an oxygen-rich atmosphere, insects with the largest fins used their fins as wings, and they survived and developed flight. So, to the gentleman who sits next to Mr. Wilberg, would you say that because insect wings were developed for a purpose different than flight, that flight is unnatural for insects?"

"No, sir," my companion asserts.

"Excellent! Therefore, could we say that flight may be possible for any creature not intended to fly?"

Five or so years later, I stand in line at Great Lakes Dragaway in Union Grove, Wisconsin.

"I'd like to enter my Norton 750cc Scrambler in today's motorcycle race," I say to a woman who sits at a table shaded by an oak. Beside her, a hand-lettered sign reads *Registration*. She wears a denim shirt and jeans. A warm wind turns the pages of a yellowed paperback novel that lies on the table next to a pack of cigarettes. She looks at me and begins to speak.

"I'm sorry, I can't hear you," I shout above the roar of two A Gas Coupes. Drivers simultaneously pump the throttle of a supercharged, big-block engine and ease the clutch to inch to the starting line. Lights similar to a traffic stoplight separate the two cars. Called a "Christmas Tree," the lights will signal the start of a thunderous sprint to the finish line one quarter mile down the resurfaced, former-asphalt county road that had been converted to a dragstrip.

"I tried to say, what's your name?" She picks up a sheet of paper and a pencil stub.

"Ah, Richard Wilberg," I say. "Call me Richard."

She reaches for a smoke, leans closer to me, and pushes the sheet of paper and pencil across the table. "Okay, honey, please fill out this registration form. Do you have a kill switch?"

"Kill switch? What's that?"

"Okay, race fans, we have a winner," the announcer blares through speakers in the grandstand.

"A kill switch, honey, cuts off your engine if you fly off your bike."

"Fly off my bike?" I jerk my head back "I don't plan to dump my motorcycle at a hundred miles per hour."

"Accidents happen, honey." She blows a blue-white smoke ring that drifts over her head. "If you lose control due to tire blowout, engine explosion, equipment failure, or any reason whatsoever, we have to protect our fans from your runaway bike."

⌒〜

In autumn 2010 or 2011, I sit in the breakfast nook at Balsam Mountain Inn in Balsam Mountain, North Carolina. I'm greeted by a staff person.

"Good morning, sir. My name is Gina, and I'll serve you breakfast. Coffee? Where are you from?"

"Coffee would be great, Gina, thank you." I place my book to the side. "I'm Richard. I live in Wisconsin."

"Wow, I'd love to go to Wisconsin." She pours my coffee. "But I've never left North Carolina, and I'm scared to death of airplanes. You know what? Someday I'm going to fly out of here."

"Oh, that's too bad." I sip my coffee. "About airplanes, I mean."

"I see you're reading Hemmingway." She sets the coffee pot on the table. "I love books.

On my break, I sit on the porch chairs and read. Not the rocking chairs. They're reserved for guests. I have a private place in back where I'm not disturbed."

"What do you read?"

"*To Kill a Mockingbird*. My son started *Moby Dick*. It was hard for him at first, but I encouraged him to read. Now he likes the story."

"You're a good mother."

"I try, but sometimes I'm not. I worked at McDonald's before here. When I came home after work, I would yell at the kids. It's better at home since I started this job. More relaxed. Momma says I should go back to McDonald's and make better money, but I like my work here."

"How big is your family?"

"My son is eleven and my daughter is eight. His name is Alexander, like Alexander the Great. Her name is Victoria. She says, not Princess Victoria, but Queen Victoria."

"Creative children," I say. "I like your Balsam Mountain Inn T-shirt. Did you buy it in the gift shop?"

"Yes. I wish I could wear a skirt with my T-shirt, but management wants me to wear jeans and sneakers. A skirt or dress would be more comfortable, especially in this heat. So, every night when I get home from work, I change into my dress and dance. You know what? Every night I fly out of here."

Pointless

I'm a teenager. I fish for smelt, a pointless recreational activity. Or is it? I sit with Davy in my kitchen. It's late afternoon in early April 1962.

"They're supposed to run tonight." He takes a deep drag on a Camel cigarette. Davy has smoked Camels for as long as I knew him. That would have been since freshman year at Nicolet. Maybe Davy smoked before that. I don't know because like many experiences in my life, I rarely probe more deeply.

I learned Davy's name when Mr. Johnson asked our gym class to line up by first name. First name? I thought all teachers and coaches had students line up by last name. Since most of us didn't know each other, we had to introduce ourselves and line up accordingly. Maybe that was his point. After about five minutes of chaos, we formed our line, and in my case, my future friend Davy stood to my left.

"Run you say?" I shake my head. "Who says?"

"Channel Four." Davy blows a perfect smoke ring between us. He pauses, shapes his lips, and releases a white dot of smoke that merges within the smoke ring.

"Those TV reporters are usually wrong," I say. "Lake

Michigan is still too cold for smelt. Channel Four gave the same report last week. We didn't catch any."

"Yeah, I know." Davy snuffs out his smoke. "You got anything better to do?"

"Nope."

"Let's go."

~

Silver, black, and iridescent, smelt belong to the *Osmeridae* family of small fish found in fresh and salt water. Abundant in the Great Lakes in the 1960s, smelt also live in the Pacific Northwest, Canada, Northern Europe, Northeast Asia, and Japan where rivers meet the sea. Construction of canals in the United States in the nineteenth century permitted ocean ships to enter Great Lakes harbors. Fish, along with smelt, followed.

Smelt run each spring like salmon or trout to streams and rivers of their birth to spawn and reproduce. Smelt are related to salmon and trout but are significantly smaller. The ones we catch rarely exceeded five inches with a diameter a bit smaller than a fine-rolled cigar. Maybe that's why we smoke stogies after we fish for smelt?

When smelt *run*, they show up in the hundreds. When they don't run, there are none. When smelt run, we net them by one of two means. Our first and quickly rejected method is to use a dragnet.

"Grab this end of the net, Dick." Davy tosses me a corner of a dragnet similar to a trawl net used by commercial fishermen but smaller. Our net measures about four feet high and ten or twelve feet wide. We wear chest-high, rubber waders and walk in Lake Michigan's forty-degree water parallel to the beach at Doctors Park in Fox Point. On a calm night, water stays in the lake where it belongs and not over the top of our waders to soak our clothing and wool underwear.

"Keep the whole net under water," Davy shouts.

I push deeper. Cold numbs my forearms. I shiver. Soon the net, loaded with fish, drags on lake bottom. We struggle to shore and dump our catch on a canvas tarp. Smelt flip and squirm in moonlight. After several trips, we estimate our catch at about half of a thirty-gallon, galvanized-steel garbage can.

"There has to be a better way," I say.

"There is." Davy laughs.

About a week later, Davy points to a newspaper ad that advertises what we need for our second method to catch smelt.

"Dip nets are on sale at Sears," he says. "I'll pick one up, and we'll fish tomorrow night. Could you round up your dad and uncle to help? We'll need extra manpower to haul our smelt home."

The next evening I stand once again chest deep in Lake Michigan. This time I grip Davy's dip net. Smelt swim below my net.

"Lower, kid," Dad shouts from the jetty. He spots smelt with his flashlight and barks orders.

I push the net down and lift a load of fish to Davy and Uncle Wally, who stand on the jetty. They dump the catch into a thirty-gallon garbage can. Davy jumps into the lake for his turn. I scramble out and shiver on the jetty. Davy, Uncle Wally, and I alternate net duty. No net duty for Dad. He usually gets what he wants.

"Okay, men, we've caught our limit." Dad shines his light on the garbage can that overflows with smelt. "Time for stogies." He bites off the end of a cigar, lights his smoke, and passes cigars to each of us. We shiver and smoke in satisfaction.

"You know," Davy says, "I heard that we're not done catching smelt until each of us bites the head off a fish and spits it into the lake." We smoke in silence.

"Who told you that?" I grumble.

"A guy from Finland."

"Finland? Who do you know from Finland? And what's the point?"

"There's no point." Davy grabs a fish and begins to chew. "It's just what smelt fishermen do."

We decline Davy's suggestion and haul our load up the hill to his pickup and head for home. At sunrise, we admire our work: cleaned smelt stuffed into milk cartons, filled with water, and ready for the freezer.

"There has to be a better way," I say.

"There is." Davy laughs. "Fresh caught smelt, already cleaned, are on sale at Red Owl for twelve cents per pound. We netted about fifty pounds. Spent three hours in the lake and another three hours cleaning them in your basement. We also lost a full night of sleep on a weeknight. I'll be late for work, and we stink like fish. Want to go again next week?"

"Maybe." I shrug.

"You got anything better to do?"

"Nope."

"Let's go."

Pork Chop

Maybe late summer 1962, I park the Green Hornet in one of the few shady spots at Bayshore Shopping Center in Glendale, south of Nicolet. I'm headed to Bob Sacks record store to pick up a new 45. A familiar face exits the store as I'm about to enter.

"Hi, Ray, I haven't seen you since high school," I say. "What have you been up to?"

"Hey, Dick, great to see you. I pick up garbage for the village."

"Really?" I offer a Lucky Strike to Ray. "By yourself?"

"Never smoked." He waves away my offer, so I light mine. "There are three of us in the crew. Mike drives the dump truck. I don't think you know him. I hang on the back of the truck on curbside. Butch stands opposite me on driver's side. You remember him from high school, right? Hey, did you hear that Butch and Betty plan to get hitched?"

"No, I hadn't." I choke in the middle of a drag.

"Yeah, real soon, shotgun and all, if you catch my drift." Ray tugs on the soiled visor of his baseball cap. "Well, back to my story. As I was about to say, when the truck stops, we jump off, head to the edge of the lawn, pick up garbage cans, and empty the contents into the back of the truck."

"Wow, those steel cans must be heavy." I flick the ash from my cig. "You like your job?"

"Yeah, they're hefty, and I have a great job except for a few things. One time when I lifted a garbage can overhead, a maggot dropped onto my cheek between my eye and my glasses. That was bad. Mike also wants to finish the route as quickly as possible. Sometimes he heads for the next stop before I'm back on the truck. If Mike speeds up too quickly, garbage falls off the truck. I have to run back to get it. But, hey, it's a steady job. I get to work outside. Mike and Butch are great friends. And I'll retire with a pension in thirty years."

Fifty-five or more years later I head out the front door of my home in Madison for my morning walk. Two blocks into my routine, I'm interrupted by screech of brakes and groan of a yellow robotic arm as it emerges from beneath a monster truck on the street in front of me. An oily, steel hand snatches a forty-eight-inch tall, plastic garbage bin that sits at the curb. *Whoosh*, the arm returns with the bin and dumps the contents into the enclosed back of the truck. The robot returns the container to the curb. Lid open, the bin bounces to the ground and dislodges the remains of my neighbor's dinner. I wave to the driver. He doesn't see me nor the pork chop on the street as he heads to the next stop.

Return of the Sun

A late summer day, perhaps in 1963 or 1964, expands before us. Dad and I stand waist-deep in the cold green water of Fish Lake in Waushara County, Wisconsin. Hundreds of suns reflect from water's dappled surface. We fish for panfish.

"I got another one, Dick." Dad's fly rod arches to point toward a hooked sunfish that swims circles beneath the water's glass-like surface. An hour later Dad's creel, a fabric pouch he straps to his waist just above water line, bulges with fish. He catches another.

"I have more room in my live bag than you have in your creel," I say.

Fly fishers might use a creel to conveniently transport a few fish. Or a catch may be corralled in a live bag that holds many fish under water. Creels are not designed to hold many fish.

"Nah." Dad unhooks his catch. "I'll just jam 'er in."

Jam indeed. When Dad pushes the fish into his packed creel, another fish is accidentally shoved out.

"Darn, one got away," he shouts.

A fish descends like a submarine when he takes water

into his bladder. To ascend, he expels water. When fish are stuffed into a creel, they gulp air instead of water. With his bladder full of air, the escaped sunfish swims on the surface of the lake. His mouth is below waterline and his back dorsal fin projects above the water's surface, not a normal behavior for a sunfish. Dad's fish swims in lazy circles around him, each circle wider than the last. Years later I will see the movie *Jaws* with the shark's dorsal fin above water. The film's drum-beat score that announces the terror of Jaws' approach will remind me of Dad's errant sunfish.

"I'll grab him." Dad reaches for the fish and misses. "He seems stunned." Now beyond Dad's reach, the fish swims toward the center of the lake.

"Looks like you lost him," I say.

"Nah." Dad looks at me. "You can't lose what you've never had."

"Look at that!" I point toward the vagabond fish. Almost beyond visibility, he turn back toward shore, slowly at first and, as seconds pass, he swims deliberately toward us.

"He's coming straight for me." Dad hands me his fly rod. "I'll catch him with my bare hands." Catch indeed. Dad scoops the wayward sunfish from the lake and returns the fish to his creel.

Forty or so years later I greet my host, Sam Smith. He and his family own and operate a northern Wisconsin resort I'll call Loon Lake Lodge. They also own and manage an adjacent golf course. "Today is a great day to fish," I say.

"Hey, Richard, leave some for me." He lifts with a bit of

effort from his director's chair and pushes his baseball cap back from his forehead. "Do you want to fish from the boat dock? I'll leave you some privacy. I've got work to do in the lodge. New guests are arriving tonight."

"Yup, just panfish today." I step onto the dock's shaky, redwood-stained wood planks six inches above the water's bronze-metallic hue. Tamarack pines line Loon Lake's shore, their tannin gives the lake its color. I carry an Orvis light-weight, fiberglass fly rod and artificial flies. Lightweight monofilament line is wound on my Orvis reel. My fish line will break with a tug from a fish larger than two pounds. My catch will have a fighting chance.

Sunfish, perch, crappies, or any kind of panfish that hide in shallow water under the dock are my goal. I'll use an artificial wet fly, hand-tied by my brother-in-law, Doug. He named the fly a Silver Nymph. Now deceased, Doug was an avid fly fisher, conservationist, and a member of Trout Unlimited, Wisconsin chapter.

Doug spent Saturday mornings in trout streams where he placed logs and branches to create nests for trout to hide and reproduce. He fished Saturday afternoons when insects hatched and dropped into the stream to provide an evening meal for hungry trout. While he fished, Doug noticed the insects that attracted the most trout. He brought specimens of these bugs home and hand tied replicas in his workshop. The Silver Nymph was born!

Silver Nymph isn't listed in an Orvis catalog of artificial wet flies, nor will most fly fishers know her characteristics. But Doug knew what trout liked to eat, and he produced a limited supply of Silver Nymphs for personal use and to share with family and friends. Fortunately for me the lure was also perfect for panfish.

I'm now a catch-and-release fisher. I fish for sport and return each fish I catch to the lake or stream. I gave up use of a live bag years ago. "Whatever you keep in a live bag, you'll have to clean," Dad used to say.

After my tenth or so cast, I hook a sunfish. He swims frantically in circles as I coax him toward me. *Bam!* A muskellunge, a game fish ten times larger than the sunfish, explodes from under the dock. The sunfish, with my Silver Nymph, disappears into the musky's cavernous mouth.

The musky slides past me, his green, lumpy, flat head, like that of an alligator, glows in the sun. The intruder vanishes as quickly as he appeared. My fly rod arcs toward the musky's retreat. Fish line zips from my reel. Within seconds my line breaks. He escapes with the unlucky sunfish.

"Lost him," I shout to no one. My fly rod clatters to the dock as I sprint to the cottage to check my tackle. How many Silver Nymphs do I have? Was the one I lost my last? I bound up the steps, two at a time. The cabin's screen door slams behind me. My tackle box yields six Silver Nymphs, each one infinitely more valuable than the one I lost.

Blindsided

On an early weekday morning before dawn in 1963 or 1964, an over-the-road diesel truck turns toward me. *Blaahh!* The klieg horn and the squeal of brakes slice through the fog. I turn my Norton motorcycle away from the truck's brilliant headlights.

"Hey kid, I almost hit you." A silhouette in the truck's window leans toward me. "What are you doing here at this time of night?"

"I work here," I shout above the noise of the truck's motor and the *pop, pop, pop* of the engine under me. "And I'm not a kid. I load trucks for UPS. I'm a Teamster, just like you. I'll probably unload your truck this morning."

"And who might you be?" The cab door opens, and he jumps down.

"Ah—Richard." I squirm on my cycle's seat, unsure if I should continue this conversation at three o'clock in a deserted parking lot.

"Good to meet you, Richard." He extends his hand to greet me. "Ralph," I think he says. I release the bike's handlebar throttle to receive his grip. My engine sputters and dies.

"Oh, great!"

"What did you say?" He steps closer, a shadow becomes a man with a grin on his broad face and a body taller, heavier, and bigger in the shoulders than mine.

"Nothing." I slide off my cycle and lean her on the kickstand. "I didn't know what to expect when I cut you off. I thought I might have to get away, the motor died, and the bike is hard to start, that's all." My voice breaks. "Sorry I blocked your way."

"Ah, that's okay. What do you do when you're not here to load trucks?"

"I'm a student at the university."

"Good for you! I've got a kid at home like you. I take extra precautions when I drive. Have to do that, you know. Could have blindsided you. Never know what I'll face in a parking lot or on a highway when I haul a load back to Minneapolis."

∽

Fifty-five or so years later, a featureless streamlined truck on Interstate Highway 94 north of Madison streaks past my Volvo XC 40.

"What's that?" I turn my head toward Wayne, who sits beside me. We're on our way back to his farm in Ashton, Wisconsin, about ten miles northwest of Madison. We've been photographing barns all morning. Another day of beautiful sunrises, "sweet light" as Wayne says.

"That could be a driver-assisted truck." Wayne removes his Wisconsin Badgers baseball cap to run fingers through his hair. "Driver-assisted cars were just the start. People couldn't imagine there might be more autonomous vehicles than just personal cars. UPS bought a fleet of driver-assisted electric trucks. Someday, freight will be delivered by robots. Do you realize there are over three million truck drivers whose jobs are at risk? Where do you think that truck was headed?"

"Has to be Minneapolis," I say.

Omega to Alpha

*D*ad and I sit at the bar at Goldenberg's in Bayshore Shopping Center. Today is my twenty-first birthday. Goldenberg's is a local watering hole operated by "Buckets" Goldenberg, the storied lineman for the Green Bay Packers.

"Take my watch, Richard." Dad opens the clasp of the white and yellow-gold link band of his self-winding Omega Seamaster wristwatch. "You're a man now." Gold numerals on the watch's pearl face gleam in the dim light. His watch slides with a gentle bump to the bar.

"Thanks, Dad." I slip part of his life onto my wrist and fasten the clasp. The face of the watch swings below my wrist. The watch pulses as I raise my hand to shake his.

"We'll get the band resized for you." He rubs my back. His strong, thick fingers feel warm through my plaid cotton shirt in the air-conditioned tavern.

"I didn't expect this." I turn to him. "You love your watch. It's part of you. I thought you just wanted to buy me a birthday drink." I lift my first legally consumed Brandy Old Fashioned in toast. Our glasses touch. "Here's to you, Dad."

~

Maybe forty years later, my fishing guide points down-stream. For this story, I'll call him Jason. He and I stand side by side in the knee-deep water of the McKenzie River in McKenzie Bridge, Oregon (within the Willamette National Forrest).

"Watch your line, Richard." Jason motions to our left. "You're almost in the rapids. Try to work your fly over by the edge of the stream. The biggest salmon hide in the pools."

"Okay, Jason."

Yellow afternoon sun glints from ripples on the water's surface. I retrieve my line and begin another cast. The waxy line moves forward and backward, forward and backward. Neither the line nor the Woolly Bugger wet fly touches the surface. Sun catches each cast, the fishing line a golden string of focus between me and the pool. Time suspends until the precise moment when I drop the fly on the pool's placid surface. A fish explodes through silence.

"Got him," I say. The tip of my Orvis fly rod points in the direction of the salmon's run. Line sings through the rod's eyelets before it goes slack. "Lost him. Why did he have to get away?"

"Come on, Richard." Jason jerks his thumb toward the pines behind us. We slosh our way to the edge of the river, climb the red clay bank studded with granite boulders, and walk among Douglas firs to camp. Jason pokes orange embers in the remains of the campfire from our earlier lunch.

"You didn't lose your fish," he says. We sit on a couple of stumps. "The fish wasn't deeply hooked. This time of the year is spawning season. Every three or four years, Chinook return to reproduce in the same stream and pool where they were born."

"Yes, we also have spawning season for trout in Wisconsin."

"Female Chinook return first. She digs a furrow with her tail fin in the bottom of the stream. The depression is called a redd. Then she lays her eggs in the redd. Soon a male appears to fertilize her eggs. She next covers her fertilized eggs with pebbles. In spawning season females won't eat and males can't eat."

"What do you mean males can't eat?"

"Male Chinook may strike your fly but not eat. His jaws are bony and twisted. He's difficult to hook. You likely irritated a male who snapped at your Woolly Bugger and spit it out. Nature curves the male's jaw so the father doesn't eat. Then he dies to make way for his young."

Let Your Future Find You

I imagine a chance encounter with my elementary school baseball coach. Perhaps we meet in the summer of 1964 or 1965. Hard to say. Every day seems the same. I aimlessly thumb through bins of 45 rpm records at Bob Sacks. Perhaps this is what happens:

"Hey, Dick, find anything good?" A hand touches my shoulder. "Do you still go by Dick?"

"Coach Wagner." I turn. "Why are you here? I haven't seen you since grade school. Actually, I prefer Richard now, but you may call me Dick if you like."

"Oh, I've seen you many times since then," he says. "You haven't noticed me. Today I stopped for groceries at Kohls, and as I walked back to my car, I saw you in the window. You looked troubled so I came in."

"Where is your food?" I grin.

"I changed my mind about shopping."

"You always seem to find me when something's wrong."

"That's what coaches do." He gestures toward two adjacent chairs. "Want to talk?"

"I was kicked out of college for bad grades, so I changed my part-time job to full time." I settle back in my chair. "In

September I'm allowed to re-enroll in school. Last week when I gave my boss a month's notice so he could hire a replacement, Red fired me. I'm nervous about college, and I'm out of work. I don't know what to do."

"How do you feel about uncertainty?" Coach scoots his chair closer to mine.

"I feel *lost*, like I don't belong at college or at Red's."

"I understand. May I be your mentor, not your coach, and share a story?"

"You are and you usually do."

"When we feel lost in life or work, our first reaction might be to rush to a solution to eliminate uncomfortable feelings." He looks at me. "Rather than focus on a quick fix, however, I suggest we prepare ourselves for a future that is beyond our imagination."

"How do I do that?"

"You let your future find you. Begin with discovery of who you are at your core, your true self or authentic self. Then try to live in accord with what you discover. If you do, you will be able to trust that you will arrive at a future you want."

"Okay, but what's my authentic self?"

"Great question. Maybe an example will help. Myths across cultures describe animals that guide humans. These tales are metaphors for when we feel lost. They describe the importance of living toward who we really are. If we do, these myths describe arrival at a future that is different from the present and rewarding for us. Are you still with me?"

"I think so, we studied myths in high school."

"Good. In the Roman myth *Romulus and Remus*, for example, twin brothers were born of a human mother impregnated by a god. Neither human nor god, the misfits were abandoned by their mother. A she-wolf found the boys and raised them. Shepherds later rescued the twins and named them Romulus and Remus. The twins ultimately established the Roman Empire. The lives of the boys were shaped by trauma as a result of human abandonment and by being raised in an alien culture represented by the wolf. Throughout their ordeal, the boys remained loyal to their humanity. They never identified with the wolf nor rejected being human. The twins endured, so when they returned to the human world, they created a future they couldn't have visualized when they were lost like you."

Last Ride

"*R*ichard, let's go see the old depot before they tear her down." Jeannie hands me the day's *Milwaukee Sentinel.* We sit in the Green Hornet at the Milky Way, a drive-in restaurant down the road from Nicolet, on an afternoon in late spring 1966.

"The last train will arrive on May 15th." Jeannie turns toward me. "The paper says the terminal will be demolished to make way for a new expressway along Milwaukee's lakefront. A freeway on Lake Michigan doesn't seem like a good idea. And why do they have to demolish a beautiful old train station?"

"I don't know." I lay the paper on the seat between us. "It's too late today and I don't have time for a visit this week. Maybe we could drive over later? The Sentinel says the new station will be nice."

"Later may be too late." Jeannie picks up the paper. "This depot was built in 1889. Milwaukee County purchased the property from Chicago & Northwestern Railroad in 1964. The terminal is described as a fine example of Romanesque architecture."

"I sort of remember the building." I lean back in my seat. "I don't know; I'm so busy."

"My family used to take the interurban train to Chicago." Jeannie slumps back in her seat. "As a child I scampered down long halls, past caged ticket counters. Laughter and games of hide and seek with my brother were the highlights of my visit. The smell of polished wood banisters and a hint of smoke and coal dust lingered in the air from the days before diesel locomotives replaced steam engines. I remember a restaurant with white tablecloths that served delicious fresh meals and wonderful bakery. The terminal is a lovely, quiet, cavernous place with inlaid tile floors, dark stained-wood walls, vaulted ceilings, and a majestic clock tower. I'd love to see the old depot one more time."

"We'll see the station later."

"Later could be never, Richard."

Over forty-eight years later, I walk to the front of the hall and face the audience for Spring Recital at Blast House Studio in Madison.

"I started my song ten or more years ago." I move to center stage, mic in hand. "On vacation in Balsam Mountain, North Carolina, I spotted a World-War-II era four-door Hudson parked at the top of a long driveway. The car faced downhill as if the driver, many years earlier, planned a trip." I walk to the Nord keyboard, adjust the bench, and sit.

"Inspired by the Hudson, I wrote lyrics first, then searched for the genre. I tried country, pop, folk, and rock. Nothing seemed to work. By accident I tried blues, and with a

few adaptations, the lyrics, melody, and music came together."
I vamp an E flat major chord for warm-up. "Composed for
piano in the key of B flat major, Last Ride verses one, two, and
three are standard eight-bar blues." I sing:

LAST RIDE
Andy Blue drove up his driveway at night.
Driving to Georgia he'll leave at first light.
Planning to travel on Tuesday at dawn,
Parking the Hudson, he cut 'cross the lawn.
But tomorrow skipped Andy Blue.

After his wake, Betty Blue took a fall.
Going to Memphis no need for it all.
Betty asked Stuart to sell Andy's car.
Stuart was drafted and left for the war.
And tomorrow skipped Betty, too.

Life's the last ride; drive it on through.
This is the day that you will do.
Take time now; don't waste it away.
Drive your car; don't wait for a day.

Today, the Hudson still waits for a ride.
Sitting in grasses, flat tires they hide.
Broken back windows are making a door,
For skunk and possum don't matter no more.
So, tomorrow skipped Hudson, too.

I could be Andy or Betty Blue.
You could be Stuart and Hudson, too.
We don't need plans for what we will do.
Don't let tomorrow skip me and you.

Life's the last ride, drive it on through.
This is the day that you will do.
Take time now; don't waste it away.
Drive your car; don't wait for a day.

When Chickens Are Wrong

I walk through an open gate onto my friend Rich's farm. Before me, like tranquil whitecaps floating on a sea of green, chickens bob and dip, bob and dip as they scratch and peck for food on his secluded hillside pasture in southwest Wisconsin. Early morning sun plays hide-and-seek with cotton-ball clouds that drift above me.

"Hey, Richard, what brings you this way?" Rich removes his work gloves and extends his hand.

"Hi, Rich." I return his handshake. "I took a shortcut home, saw you by the fence, and decided to say hello." I glance over his shoulder toward the pasture. "How many chickens do you have?"

"About thirty." Rich's bib overalls and boots are stained from morning chores. He turns toward the pasture. "Chickens are a sideline to our dairy business, but we take time to give names to most of them."

"How do you tell them apart? They all look the same."

"Well, at first, all you see is a bunch of white chickens." He rubs gray stubble on his chin, lifts an RCA portable radio from a fence post, and sets it at his feet. Elvis croons, "Love me tender."

74

"If you look closely, you'll learn differences among chickens." Rich points toward the closest birds. "See that hen with the gimpy leg? We call her Peggy. Or that one with the gray tail? Her name is Ashes."

"Yes, I see differences."

"Chickens tolerate minor differences in the flock like Peggy's limp or Ashes' gray tail. But if chickens sense a mortal difference, such as signs of a serious illness or a weakness that could decimate the population, they'll destroy the perceived threat so the flock will survive." Rich pauses. "Sometimes chickens' perceptions are wrong."

"What do you mean?"

"See this chicken feed?" He scoops his sun-tanned hand into a brown-stained metal pail. "It's grain meal with a small amount of protein and amino acids. Chickens are omnivores. They free range during the day and scratch up seeds, a few worms, and bugs. Most of their diet, however, is the meal I provide when I coop them up at night."

He tosses the feed from his hand to the delight of several birds. "One evening, when I shooed them into the coop, one of the hens scratched the skin above her eye on the chicken wire near the door. I didn't think her injury was serious and she didn't seem to be bothered by the scratch. We have one of those new recording devices in the coop to monitor for foxes. I looked at the images the next day—

"At first the other chickens near the feeder didn't notice her injury until the wound began to bleed." His knuckles turn white as he grips the pail. "Then one hen pecked her eye. Two or three more chickens attacked, and soon the injured hen wobbled away from the feeder. The aggressors followed, but not the rest of the flock. The aggressive hens pecked at the injured hen's wing feathers. In the close quarters of the coop, attacks escalated, and the wounded bird fell to the coop floor. The chickens that attacked strutted over her prone body. She died, a victim of the wrong perception."

Over thirty years later and a thousand miles from Rich's farm, a man several years younger than I, slides into the booth seat across the table from me. We sit in Amtrak's dining car, westbound to Seattle.

"I'm Arturo; may I join you?" he says. "Looks like you write music."

"Of course. I'm Richard." I turn my notebook toward him. "I compose lounge music interspersed with quick-paced house music. Are you a musician?"

The car lurches as the train leaves the station. Arturo grips the table and leans back. His close-cropped, jet-black hair gleams in afternoon sun. An onyx stud graces his right earlobe. He glances out the window.

"Montana is a desolate place," he says. "I'm a deejay and live in New York. I compose deep house music. Do you know about The Warehouse, the origin of traditional house music in Chicago? I did my best compositions in the 1980s when I lived in Chicago."

"Yes, I've heard of The Warehouse. I lived in Chicago in the late 1970s and all of the 1980s. My home is Wisconsin now. In the early 1980s, I hung out at Studebakers, a club in Schaumburg owned by Walter Payton. Dancers loved house music. They even danced on table tops. House reminds me of disco. Before house music, I danced disco until it disappeared. What killed disco?"

"Some straight, white, southern rock and roll bands and their fans perceived disco as gay music, non-mainstream, and a threat to their culture." Arturo sighs. "Do you remember a Chicago-area rock-and-roll radio station's promotional event in 1979 that urged fans to bring disco albums to a White Sox game?"

I nod my head.

"Fans were asked to stomp on the disco albums between double-header games at Comiskey Park." Arturo's eyes flick between me and distant mountains outside the window. "Promoted as 'Disco Demolition Night,' the event was a disaster. Cooped up in the close quarters of the infield, TV cameras captured fans as they shredded record album paper covers into pulp and ground vinyl disks into shards that littered the ball diamond. A riot followed, fires erupted, and police cleared the park. Officials cancelled the second game. Yes, disco died, but it was killed for the wrong reasons."

"How so? You said disco disturbed some music fans. Certainly, disco didn't threaten everyone."

"Perception, my friend. The joke's on them. Disco as a music genre died, but most of disco's style survived. Disco evolved into electronic dance music. You can't kill what people like just because of minor differences among music lovers. Music will survive."

As Usual

A man, limps down the dining car aisle on eastbound Amtrak's Southwest Chief near Albuquerque, New Mexico. The train sways and delivers him into the seat across from me.

"Howdy." He extends his hand. "I'm George. I didn't intend to sit with you, but now that I'm here—"

"I'm Richard. Please join me for lunch. How are you?"

"Not well." A frayed undershirt rings his neck. "I'm headed to Kansas to bury my mother."

"Oh, I'm sorry."

"Thank you, Richard. My biggest problem was how to find someone to care for my cats while I'm away."

"Was your mother's death unexpected?"

"Mom lived alone since the divorce." He runs fingers through thin gray hair. "I moved to Arizona years ago. Last week I had to take the cats to the vet. They're much better now. It's a big job to care for cats when you live alone." He reaches for the lunch menu sandwiched between salt and pepper shakers. A cuff button is missing from his flannel shirt.

"Did you see your mother often?"

"I used to drive sixteen hours to Kansas without a rest,

until I sideswiped a guardrail. Now I take the train. My brother will look in on the cats while I'm gone."

"Won't your family be at the funeral?"

"Mom didn't want anything special." He leans back. "Raindrop is the oldest, then Fluffy, Tiger, and Felix. I miss them already."

Another day I sit with regulars I've come to know at the EVP coffee shop on East Washington Avenue in Madison.

Billy reads the morning sports page out loud. He clears his throat and looks about.

Mike's mom purchases coffee to go. Maybe she's late for a parent-teacher conference and leaves her order on the counter.

Dan idles a city bus in a no-parking zone. He carries coffee on board while his passengers wait.

Ralph thumbs through yesterday's mail. Most are addressed to Occupant.

Senator Risser finishes a crossword puzzle. He searches the room for familiar faces of his constituents and starts another puzzle.

I sit at a table in The Pine Cone truck stop in Johnson Creek, Wisconsin, a forty-minute drive east of Madison. My server holds her order pad in her left hand, a ballpoint pen in her right. *Clara* is embroidered in script on her apron.

"You ordered the same soup for lunch last week, honey," she says.

"Yes, that's right." I look up from my menu. How nice to be remembered. "Clara, I'm Richard."

"You sat at the table by the door."

I sit upright in my chair. Maybe she likes me?

"Will you have the same sandwich today?"

"Yah, I mean yes." My heart races. I lay the menu on the table in front of her.

"Would you like your coffee now?"

"Yes." My voice is unsteady. "I'm sorry but I don't remember you."

"Don't worry, honey. I don't remember you either, but I never forget an order."

❧

I enter Bahn Thai restaurant in Madison.

"Hello, Richard." The server, whom I'll call Amara holds two menus, leads me to the center of the restaurant, and lays a single menu on a table for four. "Dinner alone?"

"As usual." I nod. "I'll have the regular please. Thanks, Amara."

"Coming right up." She hurries to the kitchen.

A silver-haired man, dressed in sport coat and slacks, sits with a young female companion, at a table to my right.

"In March 1916," he says, "Sir Ernest Shackleton led his men back from the wind-swept, 60-degree-below-zero Antarctic interior to the relative warmth of the ocean." He leans toward the woman. "Shackleton's team failed to be the first polar expedition to cross Antarctica. Instead, starvation and frostbite dogged their trek home."

"Oh, Melvin, how interesting." She touches his hand. "I love your stories. You're so smart."

"Not at all, Joyce." He grins. "You bring out my best. So, back to my story. Shackleton's ship, *Endurance*, crushed by ice, sank. Three lifeboats remained. Shackleton knew an island about 50 miles away. Darn, I don't remember the name of that island. If Shackleton and his men could row through rough seas, they might survive. Staying on the icepack meant death. They rowed. Oh, what was the name of that island?"

"Elephant," I say.

"Pardon me?" Melvin turns toward me.

"Elephant." I look at Joyce. "Elephant Island is the name of the island."

"Yes, that's right." Melvin nods. "Elephant Island. Thank you."

"Oh, you're smart too." Joyce smiles.

"For the rest of my story…" Melvin winks at Joyce. "I have etchings of the expedition to show you. Would you like to visit my apartment after dinner?"

"I'd love to." She lifts her wine glass. "To our evening."

Amara hands me my bill. "Will that be all?"

"As usual," I say.

Choice

A delicious odor of roast goat overwhelms the fragrance of cardamom infused in my Arabic coffee. I sit with a man, introduced to me as Moussa, at the entrance to his shop in City Centre, Dubai, United Arab Emirates (UAE) in 1977 or 1978.

"Ah, Friday morning in the souk offers unusual pleasures." He leans across the table and flicks an ash from his Turkish cigarette. "I observed a herd of these fine beasts on my way to meet you. Today is their turn."

Indeed, like the goats, will today be my turn? I shift position on a wood shipping crate that serves as my chair to move deeper into the shade of a frayed canvas awning.

"Ah, Mr. Wilberg. I mean no offense." He sips the remainder of his coffee, raises an arm, and waves the empty glass. A café server bows with a copper ibrik to fill his glass. Moussa nods. "Today is goat. Tomorrow maybe rugs, and the day after, we shall see. Merchants arrive at the market with similar wares on the same day. Do you see that ship in the harbor?"

I look beyond his outstretched arm as he turns toward the Arabian Gulf. Many ships line the horizon.

"Tomorrow will bring many choices." He turns back

toward me. "Shoppers will have a better chance to bargain a good price because there will be more items to purchase than buyers. But you are concerned with today. So, how may I help you, Mr. Wilberg?"

"Moussa, please call me Richard."

"Very well, Mr. Richard. May I be of service?"

"Silver," I say. "I was shown a beautiful bracelet you crafted for my associate's wife. Her husband said your work pleased her and you might make two similar bracelets for me."

Moussa's eyes drift back to the ships in the harbor. I realize my bracelets will be expensive. How expensive I will learn much later.

"Yes, that is possible." He leans back on his crate. "Please, may I show you materials and sketch ideas for how you wish your bracelets to be designed?"

"That would be good." A hot desert breeze caresses my face. He reaches below the table and lifts a black leather valise. A gleaming, pure silver ingot, the width of a fine Cuban cigar, is placed on the table. Alongside it he lays a hand-tooled leather notebook and a drawing pencil.

"May I?" I reach for the silver bar and pause.

"Of course." Moussa begins to sketch a bracelet in his notebook. "The finest silver from Morocco."

"The finest silver from the north of Spain," I say.

"No sir, Morocco." Moussa flashes a quizzical look.

"I'm having fun with you." I smile. "'The finest silver from the north of Spain' is a lyric from a popular American song by the band Looking Glass. 'Brandy, you're a fine girl. What a good wife you would be.'"

"I'm sorry, Mr. Richard, I don't know this song. Is one of the bracelets for your wife?"

He pushes his sketch across the table to me.

"No, Debbie is my girlfriend." I examine his drawing. "I love this design. Please inscribe *Debbie with Love* on the first bracelet and *Jeannie with Love* on the second."

"Ah, very good." Mousa's eyes lift from his sketch pad. "Is Jeannie your daughter, mother, or some other family member?"

"Not exactly." A cloud blocks searing desert sun from my face. "She's my other girlfriend."

"This may not be my business, Mr. Richard." He looks back at his sketch pad and exhales through pursed lips. "Do you think identical bracelets for two girlfriends is a good idea?"

"Not to worry, Moussa. Debbie lives in Chicago and Jeannie lives in Wisconsin, miles apart."

PART TWO

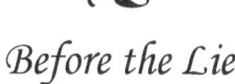

Before the Lie

Not Your Fault

*A*bout thirty years before my visit with Moussa in Dubai, maybe around my fifth birthday in 1948, I sit with my dog Pepper on the front porch of my home. We live in the 400 block of South 68th Street in West Allis, a suburb of Milwaukee.

Pepper's head warms my hand. Sunshine warms my knees. Pepper licks my cheek. A black and white Boston Bull Terrier he is, with a coat like the contents of Mommy's salt and pepper shakers I spilled on her tabletop.

Pepper stands, perks his ears, and barks at a robin across the street. I rub his velvety ears. He leaves the porch to investigate the robin. At the same time, about three blocks away, a dump truck misses its commercial destination. The driver cuts his vehicle through the neighborhood toward our home.

A week earlier, Pepper and I sat on our porch. We waited, like most afternoons, for Daddy to come home from work.

"Dicky." Daddy climbed steps two at a time and stood beside us. "I'll carry Pepper to the sidewalk so you can teach him how to come when you call." He lowered Pepper to the pavement.

"Call him," Daddy said.

"Pepper," I said.

"Say, Pepper come." Daddy nodded.

"Pepper come."

Pepper lifted his head, looked my way, and continued to sniff the grass.

"Sometimes dogs have minds of their own," Daddy said. "Try again, but louder."

"Pepper come!" He ran up the steps and sat beside me. "Pepper is a good dog."

Now, I see the truck—one block from our home. Pepper roams the neighbor's lawn across the street. Another robin alights near him.

"Pepper come."

He turns—looks at me—stalks the robin.

"Pepper come!" I stand. Truck is one-half block away.

Pepper hesitates—lopes to the sidewalk—saunters into the street.

"No, Pepper." I run down the steps. "No, no, no."

Brakes screech. Truck's right front tire rises and falls. Driver jumps from the cab. He circles the truck to face me.

"Sorry kid, I didn't see him. Your dog ran right in front of me. I couldn't stop in time."

Daddy rushes into the street. He removes his suit coat, wraps Pepper, and lays the bundle on the terrace.

"I killed Pepper." My head and shoulders shake.

"It's not your fault." Daddy holds me in his arms. "Doggies do what doggies do."

Almost a lifetime later, on another afternoon, I fly fish waist deep in Lac LaBelle in Oconomowoc, a village west of Milwaukee. My gear is by Orvis from Dad's estate, mixed with tackle I've acquired over the years. I prefer dry fly baits, usually hand-tied replicas of airborne insects, native to the location and season I fish. Purchased or hand-tied by Doug, dry flies are perfect lures. Portable and reusable, they are the best alternative to messy worms or other live baits.

After several perfect casts, I drop a caddisfly onto the mirror surface of the lake. No shadows of me or my line announce my presence. *Twitch, twitch,* concentric ripples expand with each movement of my lure. It flips right, moves left, circles right, a ballerina on a glossy stage.

A black bass, the size of a rolled loaf of country bread, laced green and black with skin texture of a submerged log, appears under my fly. The fish sucks water through torn lips. Face of scars, the old soldier's wounds testify to a life of mistakes. Each gulp brings the caddisfly closer to his cavernous mouth. He examines the fly and swims past to deeper water. Then a pause, like he has been here before. My lure wiggles and begins to lift from the pond.

The old soldier returns—lingers—advances—and rolls water's edge to barely break the surface. He swallows the fly.

I jerk the taut line that connects the caddisfly to my fly rod. A hook, hidden in the body of the lure, penetrates his gullet. He runs for deeper water. I maintain tension on the line, the tip of my fly rod arches to follow his retreat. A few more attempts to escape, and I scoop him into my net.

"It's not your fault," I whisper and let him go.

Distant World

"*H*urry up, Dicky, or we'll miss the trolley." Mommy tightens her grip on my hand and tugs me up the hill on South 68th Street.

"I don't want to go." I squint in bright morning sun. Another hot summer day in 1948.

"There's nothing to do on the trolley. I'd rather stay home and play with Bobby. He has lots of toys."

"You can always play with him." Mommy quickens her pace. "Today will be an adventure. Imagine what you'll see."

Sunlight scorches an orange and black streetcar that sits high on a hill. Wells Street trolley will transport us to downtown Milwaukee for our weekly trip to shop that may include a visit to Bitker-Gerner for new shorts and T-shirts for me. I grab the chrome railing of car number 10, quickly remove my overheated hand, and climb three steps to the coach. I lean against Mommy and kick the base of the fare box.

"Fare please." The motorman touches his leather-gloved hand to the visor of his cap. Mommy removes her spotless, white-cotton gloves. She reaches for a coin purse that hangs within the folds of her dress. She drops the token she has gripped in her left hand into the fare box and guides me forward with her right. *Crunch*. I slouch into a yellow wicker seat at the rear of the trolly, enveloped in an earthen odor of dried grass and sweat.

All seats face east, the direction of travel. The trolley lurches forward as electric current surges from the overhead power line into the dynamo engine that propels the car to our destination. I feel vibration from the motor, sit up, and look toward the window.

"The air is stuffy in here." Mommy reaches to lower the transom window. *Thud*. The steel-framed window drops open. "There, now we'll smell lake breezes."

Instead of the wet, sweet fragrance of Lake Michigan, I sense nitrogen and sulfur from electric sparks that tickle my nose as the streetcar's power transom fights to stay in contact with the overhead energy line. I want to sneeze but laugh instead.

"Thirty-fifth Street," the motorman says. I stand.

"No, not yet." Mommy pulls me back into the seat. "We'll be there soon."

A sea of workmen, their bare arms poking through blue overalls, board the trolley and flow to open seats. I stare at short-cropped hairs on the back of the neck of the man seated in front of me. His skin glistens with sweat like the shine on the trolley's wicker seat. On the back of his seat are stained shadows of workmen who sat there before. I bounce up and down. Mommy touches my shoulder.

"Thirteenth Street." The motorman turns toward the men who surge like a tide off the streetcar.

"There, that's better." Mommy closes the window.

"Third Street, everyone off." The motorman walks toward the back of the trolley that will become the front of the streetcar on the westbound return trip. As he walks, he flips the back of each seat on the left side to face west.

"Let's help the motorman," Mommy says. She moves ahead of me and begins to reverse seats on the right side of the aisle.

I leap from my seat and struggle to flip a seat on the left side. *Clunk.* The seatback faces me. Stains of grime, shadows of yesterday's army of workmen march into memory.

∿

"Daddy, I want a new toy truck." I play in my sandbox behind our home one week after my trolley ride with Mommy.

"Why?" He looks down at me. Black shoes shine in morning sunlight.

"I want to play construction with a truck."

"You have a truck."

"No, I don't."

"Yes, you do." Daddy kneels beside me. "Let me show you." Blue-pinstriped trousers depress the sand beneath his knees. He holds my right hand and guides my palm across the sand. The surface is damp and cool. As he pushes my hand, waves of sand flow to each side. Like a boat creates a wake through a lake, sand forms curbs on both sides of a flattened roadbed beneath my palm.

"*Varoom*," he says as he releases my hand. "Do you hear the truck's motor? You have everything you need." He stands and brushes sand from his pants. Wet circles of love cover both knees. "Have fun with your new truck."

I wave goodbye. *Varoom!* My hand moves through the sand toward a toy shovel that will be a trolley. I pick up workmen from the streetcar and drive them to a construction site in the center of the sandbox. My left hand, now a steam shovel, drops sand onto the back of my right. I truck the load to build a city in a distant world on the far side of the sandbox.

Reason to Call

I stand on the sidewalk below Bobby's home on a waning day of summer. Could be 1948.

"Call for Bobby, call for Bobby, call for Bobby." I will be heard.

Bobby's mommy pulls back curtains and opens the window.

"Call for Bobby, call for Bobby, call for Bobby."

"Yes, I hear you," she shouts through the window and then opens the door. "What's the reason for your call, Dicky?"

"Could Bobby come out to play?" I stretch my legs up the steps and stand beside the door.

"Of course he will." She sighs. "You don't need to call, Dicky. Next time just knock like everyone else."

Over twenty-five years later, maybe summer 1975, my finger spins the metal dial of a rotary telephone in Chicago. *Ring, ring, ring* on the other end. The phone's receiver is slippery in my shaky hand. Why is it so hot? No wonder she's not home. Maybe this time Debbie will answer.

"Hello, this is Debbie. Who's calling?"

"Hey, Debbie, it's Richard. I tried to call all evening—ring, ring, ring, you know, no one there."

"Hi, Richard. So nice to hear from you."

"Well, I thought I'd give you a buzz. No reason to call really. I just wanted to talk."

"You don't need a reason to call, Richard. If you want to talk, that's good enough for me."

Over thirty-five years later, perhaps 2011, I call Pete from my home in Madison.

"Hello, this is Pete," he answers.

"Hi, Pete, it's Richard."

"Yes, I know it's you, Richard. I see your name on my phone. I'm about to catch the news and write a note to get more eggs. And I'm ready to eat breakfast. What's up, bro?"

"Not much, Pete. I just wanted to talk."

"Hey, man, got—to—go or I'll burn these eggs. Next time before you call, Richard, text me the reason for your call."

Dirty Bunny

At five or six years of age, I played with a flop-eared, matted-cotton, one-eyed, stuffed rabbit. I named him Dynamite. Before being beat up, half-eyed, and my best friend, I called him Bunny. Just one of many ordinary stuffed animals I kept in my bedroom toy box.

On Saturday evenings in winter, Daddy entertained my sister and me at our home with *Kiko the Kangaroo* movies. He projected films onto a portable screen in our living room. For each movie, I snuggled with my stuffed animals, including Bunny. We watched Kiko's nemesis, Foxy Fox, dash from his cave to pounce upon baby birds and chase other vulnerable animals for his wicked delight. Kiko always rescued terrified victims. At the very last minute, he foiled Foxy Fox. I imagined Foxy Fox lived in our basement where Daddy stored his movie projector.

One Saturday night, just before movies, Mommy asked me to fetch a jar of peach preserves. I trembled. Peaches were stored in the basement. A good boy would retrieve a jar but only with protection against Foxy Fox. Could I rely on Kiko to rescue me? Unsure, I ran to my room and grabbed Bunny. He would help me like Kiko might, using sticks of dynamite to eliminate Foxy Fox. With that decision, Bunny became Dynamite.

☙

About a month later, I stood beside Mommy in our basement laundry room.

"How did Dynamite get so dirty?" Mommy asked as she tossed him into her bright white, post-World War II Bendix washing machine for a routine bath.

I shrugged. Monthly washes had stripped his original golden-brown bunny fur from two locations on his prematurely bald head. Yellow straw stuffing, his rabbit innards, protruded from a buff-colored body bag.

Mommy left the room for chlorine bleach. I pulled a bench close to the washer. White knuckles gripped the edge of the Bendix. My heart raced as I watched Dynamite's brown head dip and bob, dip and bob below sudsy waves. "Hold your breath, Dynamite. Maybe if I help you learn how to swim—"

"Stay back from the washer, Dicky." Mommy pulled my arm from the Bendix and lifted me down from the bench. "The agitator will rip your arm off." She closed the washer's lid and walked me out of the room.

"He'll drown, Mommy." I wiped tears from my eyes.

"No, Dynamite will be fine." She knelt beside me. "You named him Dynamite because he's strong."

An hour later we returned to the Bendix. Mommy's swift action saved my arm, but Dynamite lost his right eye. Apparently, agitators rip off more than arms.

Mommy fetched the rolling pin that earlier this month rolled cherry pie crust for a dinner dessert. "Poor baby," she said, pushing it over Dynamite's wet body. The white terry-cloth towel she placed under him absorbed clear water that squeezed out. "We'll make him a new eye after he hangs on the clothesline to dry." She patted my shoulder.

Later that day, I found a sun-warmed, fluffy Dynamite propped on my bedroom pillow. I smelled bleach, lemons, and straw as I touched the spot absent his eye where Mommy had sewn an "X" with black thread. My comic books showed dead animals with black cross-marks in place of eyes. The agitator must have killed Dynamite, too. So what? Even if he were dead, I reasoned, Dynamite would come back to life in my arms. I remembered how Foxy Fox would return each Saturday after he was killed by Kiko the week before.

Or Dynamite may have died a week before his bath when I threw him from the back window of Daddy's Oldsmobile. We were headed to grandma's house. "Stop, Daddy." I grabbed his shoulder. "Dynamite jumped out the window."

Daddy wheeled to the side of the street, ran up the sidewalk, retrieved the dirty bunny from curbside debris and handed him to me. "Jumped, huh?" He smiled and rubbed my disheveled hair.

∽

In early June 1949, we moved from West Allis to our new home at the corner of North Navajo and Willow Roads in the rural Town of Milwaukee. Summer days seemed endless. My high point of each day was the arrival of the postman. One late summer afternoon, I lay on the lawn and balanced Dynamite on my knee. I never received any personal mail except birthday cards addressed to my parents. Collecting mail was my job. I felt older with this responsibility.

I anticipated the roar of the mailman's World War II military Jeep that had been converted into a postal delivery vehicle. With letters and packages jammed to the roof, he barely had enough room to sit and steer to the opposite side of our country road. Once in position he would reach through his window to stuff our mailbox.

While I waited the sun played hide and seek with clouds. We didn't watch movies in the summer, so viewing clouds was my daily entertainment and boyhood meditation. Suddenly, Dynamite slipped from my knee and tumbled to the grass. Dappled sunlight danced across his face. A canopy of beech-wood leaves above me filtered sunlight. Shadows darted to give a semblance of animation to Dynamite's one good eye. He seemed to wink at me as if to say, "Foxy Fox is gone. You'll be fine. Time to move on."

I got up from the lawn and walked to my room. I laid Dynamite in my toy box and sprinted to the garage for my baseball and glove. The mitt was soft and warm, a bit too large for my hand but of a size and a challenge I would grow into. I pounded the ball into the oiled leather mitt. A pocket formed above Joe Adcock's name stenciled into the palm.

The postman shouted from his Jeep, "Hey, Dicky, you've got mail. It's addressed to you."

Mentor

"*M*ommy, who's that man on the airplane wing in the jungle?" I point to a black and white photograph in our leather-bound family album.

"Why, Dicky, that's your Uncle Wally in Burma." Mommy rubs my shoulder. "You remember him."

"Is it hot in Burma?" I try to reconcile the photograph of a shirtless teenager in fatigue pants with the man who visits us on weekends.

"Yes, it's very hot. Uncle Wally served in the Army Air Corps. He repaired airplanes."

"What's that word on the airplane?" I squint at the photo. "I can spell the word *P i s o n y a*. What does it mean?"

"Ask your father." Mommy blushes.

I didn't ask. Years later I would understand why Mommy didn't explain the meaning of *Pisonya*. Uncle Wally's team of Army airmen painted their off-color remark on the cowl of a North American Aviation B-25 bomber to taunt the enemy. Even more years later, I would learn that in addition to repairing airplanes shot by enemy artillery, Uncle Wally had another job. He cleaned up any remains after bodies were removed from planes. I always knew Uncle Wally was special.

⌒

A few weeks after I discover the photograph, Uncle Wally arrives at our home early on a Saturday morning. He will help Mommy with her work and mentor me to be more than my father's son.

"Ready to *Simoniz* your mother's car, Dicky?" Uncle Wally grins.

"I don't know how," I say.

"Watch me," Uncle Wally says. He cleans the driver's side mohair upholstery in her Chevy coupe. He flips me a sponge, and I follow his instructions on the passenger's side. Years later I will learn that Simoniz is the name of a product and not a verb for cleaning car seats.

While we work, Daddy sharpens the blade on a gasoline-powered Toro lawnmower manufactured in Minneapolis. Then he fills the mower with gas. He begins at the edge of the lawn and mows in large concentric circles. Each time he passes the point where he started, the circle becomes smaller. Years later Toro will be purchased by an international company and mowers will be manufactured overseas. I will remember our Toro.

While Daddy works and before Mommy's car seats are dry, Uncle Wally shows me how to wax her car's exterior. He rubs Blue Coral carnauba wax over the car's body in small overlapping circles that resemble dusty fish scales. Uncle Wally works outward, each small circle combined with the others in a pattern that grows larger. He knows when to remove the film. Buff too soon and the wax will streak. His test of success will be my ability to see my reflection on the hood of her car.

"Wow, I see the world," I say. "I didn't know I could do this."

As we admire our work, Daddy finishes his job. He stands in the center of the mowed lawn. His mower is out of gas.

～

In early autumn Uncle Wally shows up on another Saturday morning. "Ready to learn how to string a bow and shoot an arrow, Dicky?"

While we work, Daddy rakes leaves. He begins at the edge of the lawn and rakes leaves into a pile in the center. Then he gathers leaves in a bushel basket that he hauls to the corner of our lot. He burns leaves in solitude.

On subsequent weekends Uncle Wally teaches me how to hunt, fish, and trap muskrats. Later that year, after we are successful on our trap line, we skin our catch and stretch their pelts on metal frames. We hang the pelts like smelly, furry shirts on Mommy's basement clothesline, much to her dismay.

In November, after our pelts are cured, we pile our prizes in a corner of the basement. Before winter we will sell our cache to a furrier in Milwaukee who will transform our work into winter gloves for the needy.

～

Four or so months later, on another Saturday morning perhaps in spring 1950, Mommy pushes back our kitchen window curtains and lifts the sash. "Hey there, brother. Where have you been?"

"Hi, Helen. I've been busy. Is Dicky out of the sack?"

"Dicky, Uncle Wally is here."

I sprint through the back door, the screen banging behind me, and leap into his open arms.

"Hey, Spider." He smooths the cowlick in my hair. Years later in high school, I will try to flatten my embarrassment with Butch Wax. Disobedient hair will pop right back up like it always does.

"Good to see you," Uncle Wally says. "Today we will build a kite."

"A kite? Why don't we just buy one?"

"Oh, no, much better to build a kite." He takes my hand, and we head for the basement.

"You'll see."

To build a kite from scratch is complicated. First, we scavenge parts. Uncle Wally values reuse of materials. He grew up in The Great Depression. We fashion rough-cut wood staves from furnace room construction debris. Staves make the kite's frame. We bend a stave into a beam with string; that will be the kite's horizontal arm across a vertical stave similar to a mast on a boat. We then adhere the beam to the vertical stave and connect the four corners of the diamond-shaped perimeter with string. Next, we lay wet newspaper over the kite's frame and adhere the paper to the perimeter string with library paste.

"A kite is like a boat's sail in addition to the beam and mast." Uncle Wally points to the frame, the skeleton of his idea. "The paper drapes over the bow in the beam to provide the right amount of surface for wind to lift the kite. With too much bow, the kite will spiral down to an unfortunate crash. Too little and the kite won't climb."

Then we tie together dust cloths, pillaged like pirates

from Mommy's rag bin, to create the kite's tail. "If the tail is too long, drag will prevent the kite's climb," Uncle Wally says "Too short and the tail will follow her to a fatal crash. Paper and glue will dry overnight. Our maiden flight will be tomorrow."

∾

The next day I sprint into an early morning breeze toward distant trees at the end of a mowed lawn at Brown Deer Park, about four miles from my home.

"Run!" Uncle Wally shouts above the wind.

Our kite careens right and left above my head. Taut paper snaps, wind pulls on my arm awkwardly extended behind me.

"Let go!" he yells.

I can't. The kite might crash. My gut churns. If the wind is too strong, feeble paper will be torn to shreds. If the wind is too weak, there won't be enough lift and she will crash. Either way, all our work will be lost.

"Now!" Uncle Wally runs up behind me.

Trees loom larger. Individual pines are visible instead of the indistinguishable green swath I observed at the start of my dash. Now's the time. I clench my teeth and let go. She climbs like an airplane above me.

Uncle Wally grabs the kite's spool of twine that bumps along the lawn. He wraps the string around my hand. Wind pulls my arm skyward like an adult lifts a fallen child. Taut twine jerks and presses grooves in my hand. Paper snaps and sings as our creation soars beyond the sun.

Cool Dude

"Daddy, will we fish this weekend?" I sit at our kitchen table between him and Uncle Wally on a summer morning in 1950. We have family conversations in the kitchen—good and bad.

"I don't know, Dicky." Daddy looks past me toward Uncle Wally. "I have to mow the lawn and change oil in the Oldsmobile."

"Wes, you gave another excuse to the kid last week." Uncle Wally reaches for the coffee pot and refills his cup. "I'd like to go fishing too, Wes, and it's already a month past opening weekend. Pretty soon the weather will be too hot, and fish won't bite. We've talked about fishing for months."

"I know that, Walt." Daddy reaches for an ashtray. He rolls his flannel shirt sleeves above his muscular forearms and lights a Lucky Strike. "The house also needs painting, and Helen wants me to spade the flower beds. I can't do those jobs in winter."

"Wes, you always have some reason to change your mind." Uncle Wally pushes his chair back from the kitchen table. Blue veins pulse on his forehead. He pulls his khaki undershirt away from his neck. "You promised us that we'd

104

fish after we top-coated the asphalt driveway. That was three weeks ago."

I swing my head from Uncle Wally to Daddy, like I do when I watch them play a game of ping-pong in our basement. I fidget in my chair. They've had similar arguments before. Although Daddy usually is loudest, more physical, and seems to win the fight, Uncle Wally will ultimately settle their conflicts in more subtle ways. Years later, for example, he will draw a cartoon of a basement ping-pong game depicting a teenage me defeating Dad twenty-one to nothing. His cartoons over the years will illustrate Dad as short, balding, older, and overweight. Uncle Wally and I will be drawn as tall, handsome, youthful, and slim. On occasion he will sign his art as Black Walt, signaling his dark sense of humor.

"Plans change, Walter." Daddy snuffs out his smoke, stands, knocks the kitchen chair backward to the floor, and leaves the room.

Maybe two weeks later, I hobble across the sand at a stone quarry near Okauchee Lake, about thirty-five miles west of Milwaukee. I fall into Mommy's arms. "He bit me." A red and blue welt throbs on my left foot.

"How did this happen, Dicky?" She wipes sand from my foot and inspects the injury.

Daddy fishes beyond a bank of cattails near where we sit. He stands in the lake and wears rubber fishing boots.

"A crab bit me." I sniff back my tears, try to stand, and immediately sit back down.

"There aren't any crabs in the stone quarry, darling." She pulls me closer. "You probably had a run-in with a crawfish. What did he look like?"

"He was green with huge pinchers, like those lobsters in the tank at the supper club, except he was much smaller." I rub my toe. "I know there aren't any lobsters here, so what's a crawfish?" I watch Daddy reel in his fish line, inspect the bait, and take a cast toward the shallows. With each cast, he steps backward, farther away from where we sit.

"Grandma called them crawdads when she lived in Minnesota." Mommy laughs and adjusts her white sailor hat to shield sun from her eyes. "They're related to lobsters. Around here, dear, they're known as crawfish or crayfish. What's important to remember is a crawfish would rather get away than have an encounter with you. Although he walks forward, he avoids danger when he uses his tail to rapidly swim backward."

Daddy takes another cast and moves farther down the shoreline.

"Why does Daddy fish alone?" I turn toward Mommy. "Doesn't he want to be with us on the blanket?"

"He's not alone, darling." She smiles. "We are here on the shore close to him. He just likes to be by himself."

Sometime later, perhaps on a Saturday morning in late winter 1951, I sit on a stool at a lunch counter between Daddy and Uncle Wally. We have stopped for breakfast at Ace Diner on Bluemound Road in Milwaukee. My feet dangle above the floor like tetherballs at the end of skinny ropes swinging in the wind at my playground.

Daddy and Uncle Wally dunk cake donuts into brown-stained white mugs of steaming coffee. Across the counter a neon sign glows in early morning light. *Hills Brother's Coffee*, the sign advertises. I dunk half of a glazed donut into a glass of milk, just like a man.

"Dicky, please pass the cream." Uncle Wally gestures and leans forward to look past me toward Daddy. His voice is quiet, yet firm. "I feel bad about the sailor we cheated."

"Why?" Daddy says. "He said he wanted a low mileage car. That's what I sold him, thanks to you."

Another argument. I settle lower in my seat. When I sit between them and tempers flare, I know when to disappear.

"I'm not sure about that." Uncle Wally shakes his head. "Being a vet myself, I don't think it's right to take advantage of discharged war vets with a wad of cash and a need for a used car. The other night I attached the electric drill to the speedometer cable to set back mileage for another customer. I left the drill on too long and turned the car's mileage past zero to 90,000 miles. I had to reverse the drill and add 20,000 miles back onto the car's odometer to give the customer a low mileage automobile."

"Wally, you probably helped the customer because when he goes to sell the car, it will be worth more."

"How so?" Uncle Wally says.

"Look at it this way," Daddy answers. "There's a shortage of cars and many buyers. Low mileage cars are in demand. We help vets get reestablished. Times are tough. Remember, you have rent to pay, and I have Helen and kids to support. There's more than one way to look at things, you know."

"Yes, we have to make a living," Uncle Wally says. "But when you say the customer will get more for his car when he sells, that doesn't make sense. How does anyone win when someone else loses?"

About seven years later, I will watch Uncle Wally sketch a cartoon after a series of basement dart games among Uncle Wally, Dad, and me. Uncle Wally will make his point.

Sixty-five or so years later, maybe 2016, I sit on a stool at my kitchen table in my Madison home with Wayne. We thumb through a box of old family photographs.

"Who's the cool dude in front of the airplane, Richard?" Wayne lifts a black and white print from the box.

"That's my dad." I reach for the photo. "The plane in the background is a commercial carrier. Dad flew small aircraft after this photograph but nothing this large. He used to dream he could fly his living room chair before he obtained a private pilot's license. He flew out of Timmerman Field in Milwaukee where he met Art Zander, the TV 4 weatherman who owned a Piper Cherokee. Dad would passenger with Art or rent a Cessna 150 when he wanted to fly on his own."

"Was your father a good pilot?"

"Sort of. He had trouble with landings."

"Landings are the most important part of flight."

"For sure. *Tora! Tora! Tora!* Like a WWII bomber dives toward an American aircraft carrier."

"I saw that movie."

"Right. Dad didn't believe in slow landings. He should have been a helicopter pilot.

Mother had one flight with him. I asked why she didn't fly with him more often. She said she didn't like to fly."

About two years later, I sit with Wayne in his home.

"Richard, look at these photos." Wayne slides three 8x10-inch black-and-white prints across the kitchen table.

"Ugly!" I lay the pictures side by side. "Dead or does he play possum?"

"Last week I walked Nobu up the path we normally take for him to do his doggie duties." Wayne waves toward his back door. "Suddenly, Nobu made a beeline for the barn. I called, and he wouldn't return. I saw him circle an object on the ground near the barn. I walked over and smelled the stench before I saw the body. Phew, almost made my stomach turn."

"So, the possum was dead." I push the photographs back to Wayne.

"Well, as you see in this picture," Wayne says, "with matted fur, eyes wide open, and a tongue that hangs from his mouth, he looks dead. I lifted Nobu and walked to the barn for a shovel. When I returned to bury the body, the possum was gone."

"No way! Play acting."

"Seems that way. Although possums resemble a cross between a rat and woodchuck, they are neither rodent nor mammal. Did you know that the North American possum, also known as an opossum, is the only North American marsupial? Like a kangaroo, baby possums are called joeys. They hide in their mother's pouch to nurse and develop. When they are ready for the world, they climb out and ride their mother's back until independent."

"Yeah, but I still don't like them."

"I know. Possums have a bad rap because of their rat-like appearance, their ability to play dead, and how they mimic rotten flesh. However, an average possum eats over five thousand ticks a year. Many of these ticks carry Lyme disease. Possums are also fiercely loyal. They protect home and family before themselves. Possums are not all bad."

"Cool dude," I say.

Search Until We Find

"*H*ush, child, you'll wake the chickens." Mokey tugs my hand. The spring-hinged, pine-planked door of my maternal grandmother's chicken coop closes silently behind us as we enter. The coop is located behind her rooming-house-style home in the 4000 block of West Lincoln Avenue in Milwaukee where she raised eleven children with her husband Panteleimon. He goes by Panko. Mokey's given name is Mary, but the family calls her Mokey. Names confuse me.

The evening is warm, perhaps in late spring 1951. Temperature in the coop increases with each step we take deeper into the chicken's abode. Moonlight outside the coop yields to darkness within. "Squawk!" The monsters perched above me warn about our intrusion into their fecund solitude. I smell their feathers and feel heat like I do when I sleep in Mokey's bed under her feather-packed comforter.

"Mokey, are chickens eagles?" I snuggle up to my grandma.

"Such a question, Grandson." Her warm hand guides me deeper into the coop. "Of course not."

"Uncle Bobby says eagles drop from the sky to snatch little boys."

"He tries to scare you. Now, hand me your flashlight."

"Mokey, I want to go home." A thousand red eyes stare down on me through the flicker of the yellow beam. "Please, could we go?"

"It's okay, Dicky. Stay close to me. Give me your hand. Each day we must gather the eggs." Mokey's thin hand guides my trembling fingers beneath each monster's smooth breast.

Warm like my mother's hand, feathers caress the top of mine. "Squawk," a chicken responds.

"Mokey, I can't find an egg."

"Continue to search, Dicky. You'll find what you want."

"It's hot, Mokey." The firm object of my search brushes my palm. I slip my prize into her apron pocket.

"Ishchite, poka my ne naydem," Mokey says. Years later I will translate her words.

Twenty-five or more years later, maybe 1977, I sit at a table at the Billy Goat Tavern on lower Wacker Drive in Chicago. Billy Goat is the place to drink lunch if you are in the newspaper business, want to see and be seen, and are on the lookout for your next story. A reporter at the *Chicago Sun Times*, whom I'll call Jerry, sits on my right, and a reporter at the *Chicago Tribune*, whom I'll call Roger, sits across the table. Kathy, an account manager at D'Arcy MacManus Advertising, sits to my left. She just introduced me to Jerry and Roger to get some publicity for my urban design projects. I work at DeLeuw, Cather and Company as an urban planner. The conversation abruptly shifts from me to them.

"Hey, Roger, how's your progress?"

"What the hell do you think, Jerry." He rubs his forehead. "Chief wants my column by four o'clock. It's close to one, and I don't have a single new idea. I hate my daily grind. I wish I hadn't switched from breaking news to writing a daily column. I thought writing features with a byline would be a promotion. I could put more about myself in my column than I could in news reports.

"'Here kid, take this lede,' Chief used to say. I did that. I reported and met my deadline. Now I have to be creative every day. No one hands me a new idea like Chief did. Do you realize how hard it is to write something original every day?"

"Come on, let's have another round." Jerry waves for the server. "I've been at this job long before you were born." He winks at me.

I nod back. Roger and I are about the same age. Jerry seems like a mentor with a message I need more than publicity.

"Roger, to get where we want to be, we need to let go of what holds us back." Jerry looks at everyone at the table.

"What do you mean?" Roger pipes in.

"You said you thought your feature column could be more about you than beat reporting. What prevents you from writing from your personal perspective?"

"I'm afraid I don't have anything new to say," Roger says. "Every story has already been written. What could I add that would be of interest to my readers?"

"Yes, it's true that most topics have been covered by other writers. But there is only one you, with your perspective. You have a thousand ideas within you. Each is uniquely yours, yet part of a universal human consciousness. Grab an idea. When you risk and share your thoughts, your stories will resonate with readers who have similar experiences. Trust your intuition. Trust your writing. Reach beyond your fear."

On a Sunday afternoon in late winter 2015 or 2016 and over a hundred miles from the Billy Goat, I sit at a Kawai keyboard. Today is spring music recitals at Blast House Studio.

"Hey, folks, great to be here." I turn toward the audience. "I'm Richard Wilberg. I started my singer-songwriter career in the 1970s. I began piano lessons about five years ago. My performance today is titled 'Search Until We Find.' I was inspired to write this song by my grandmother who spoke to me in a strange blend of English and her native Russian language. My song is composed for piano in the key of C major. Here's what Mokey wanted me to know."

> SEARCH UNTIL WE FIND
> I need a new idea, to meet my daily score.
> I sift through the ashes of what I've done before.
> To face every day, a curious way.
> The gamble that I play, the risk I will pay.
>
> A story of mine, my song without rhyme.
> A waltz out of time, the mountain that I climb.
> With faith that is blind, to walk one more time.
> Ishchite poka my ne naydem.
> We search until we find.

What's True

"*H*urry, Dicky, or you'll be late for school." Momma smiles and hands me a lunchbox decorated with Donald Duck.

"I'm proud of you," she says. "A third-grader, able to walk to school alone. Come straight home after school. Uncle Wally will be here for an early supper." She points to a calendar on the wall. Let's assume September 9, 1952, is circled in red. "Follow the road. Don't cut through the field past the old barn. It's too dangerous." She pats my shoulder and nudges me out the door.

I follow the road to school. After school I'm eager to read my *Flash Gordon* comics so I take the shortcut through the field past the old barn to get home. When Flash Gordon faces danger, like Ming the Merciless on planet Mongo, I will too.

Mowed lawns yield to waist-high prairie grass. To clear the way with my right hand, I grip Donald Duck in my left. Sharp-edged grasses bloody my hand. Oh, to have a machete like *Jungle Jim*. I see the barn on a hill, two doors ajar. An iron beam projects above a hayloft entrance. A tattered rope hangs from a rusty pulley, a metal hook at the end.

My hands tremble in warm afternoon sun. Will the

farmer be at work near the barn? Is he the danger Momma warned of? I veer away from the barn, down the gully toward the creek.

Voices, indistinct at first, slow my progress. Two men dressed in overalls and work boots sit beside a fire. One seems to be older than the other. He roasts a small animal and smokes a cigarette. Men's magazines, like *Argosy* or *Esquire*, the kind I'm not allowed to read, lay by the fire next to a bottle of what looks like brandy.

"Hey, kid, want a drink?" The younger man lifts a chipped metal cup. "Squirrel will be done in a few minutes." The older man turns the roast. The creature's eyes, red like the coals beneath him, stare at me. "Come sit with us while he cooks. We'll have some fun."

The younger man chuckles.

I sprint toward the creek. Tears blur my vision. I stumble, fall, and skin my knee. Prairie grass thins to willows at creek's edge. Sapling roots project from a steep bank on the far side. I climb with both hands. Donald Duck tumbles behind me. I lose my grip—slide backward—hit my head—darkness—cold water seeps into my tennis shoes.

I run back toward the barn. The men are gone. No remains from the fire. I run past the barn, find the road, race home, and burst into the kitchen.

"Dicky, what happened?" Momma wraps me in her arms. "Where's your lunchbox?"

"I lost it. The men. They scared me."

"What men?" She dries my eyes and holds me tighter.

I tell her what happened.

"Dicky, are you sure? You have a vivid imagination. Did you make up this story because you lost your lunchbox? Now go to your room and remember what really happened. I want to know what's true."

◠

Later…

"Hurry, Dicky, or you'll be late for school." Momma smiles and hands me a lunchbox decorated with Mickey Mouse. "I can't find Donald Duck. Come straight home after school."

I follow the road to school but take the shortcut to get home. I see the barn on a hill. I veer away from the barn, down the gully toward the creek. Voices slow my progress. A boy and a girl lie on the grass in front of me.

"Get off of me." She struggles beneath him.

"Come on, I'll be your boyfriend." He laughs.

I sprint toward the creek. Prairie grass thins at creek's edge. Sapling roots project from a steep bank on the far side. I climb with both hands. Mickey Mouse tumbles behind me. I lose my grip—slide backward—hit my head—darkness—cold water seeps into my tennis shoes.

I run back toward the barn. The boy and girl are gone. No remains from their presence. I run past the barn, race home, and burst into the kitchen.

"Dicky, what happened?" Momma wraps me in her arms. "Where's your lunchbox?"

"I lost it. The boy and girl. They scared me."

"What boy and girl?" She dries my eyes and holds me tighter.

I tell her what happened.

"Dicky, are you sure? Did you make up this story because

you lost your lunchbox? Now go to your room and remember what really happened. I want to know what's true."

⁓

Later…

"Hurry, Dicky, or you'll be late for school." Momma smiles and hands me a lunch box decorated with Porky Pig. "I can't find Mickey Mouse. Come straight home after school."

I follow the road to school but take the shortcut to get home. I veer away from the barn, down the gully toward the creek. Voices slow my progress. I stop, reverse my course, run past the barn, race past school, follow the road to home, and burst into the kitchen.

"Dicky, what happened?" Momma wraps me in her arms. "Put Porky Pig in the sink."

Be Prepared

I sit in front of Mrs. Chapman's fireplace at a Cub Scout meeting on a winter afternoon. She's my den mother and Pete's mom. They live on North Seneca Road, two houses north of my friend Jimmy's home and about two blocks from my house on North Navajo Road.

"Dicky, what does it mean for a Cub Scout to be prepared?" Mrs. Chapman nods to me. I tug on my blue Cub Scout shirt collar and blue-and-yellow scout bandana that chafes my neck. Last night I studied the Cub Scout manual. I want to advance from a Tiger to a Wolf Scout. Does Mrs. Chapman ask what I need to know to become a Wolf Scout? Do I need to show how to tie a square knot, pitch a tent, fold a flag, or ford a steam? What does she want to hear? What's the right answer?

∾

Over forty-five years later, Dad and I relax in his living room. I often see Mom and Dad on weekends. No special reason for today's visit, so I'm surprised by the turn in our conversation.

"I'll be around for a long time, Dick." Dad shifts his

position in the leather easy chair to face me. "I don't want you to worry. We should discuss how I want to die. I don't want to hang around with an extended illness. I don't want to suffer or to be a burden for you kids. When the time is right, I just want to die."

My belly churns as Dad speaks the unmentionable word. Today is a beautiful spring day. We should be discussing fishing rather than his eventual demise. We don't talk about death in our family. Mother admonishes us to speak only of nice things. Dad's future death seems like a remote possibility. His active lifestyle isn't compatible with a conversation about end of life on a day like today.

∾

A few years later, on a cold April afternoon in 2004, I stand outside the emergency room at UW Hospital in Madison.

"Pneumonia is a comfortable death." The emergency room physician looks at his clipboard avoiding eye contact with me. "Most of your dad's systems have shut down. He has an embolism in his gut and kidney failure. We could give him penicillin to cure his pneumonia. Then he would return to the nursing home until something else brings him back here. It's really about his quality of life. We could keep him alive, Mr. Wilberg. What does your father want?"

Want? I turn from the doctor to look out an adjacent window and remember my earlier conversation with Dad. He knew exactly what he wanted.

"It asks on this healthcare power of attorney form if I want chest compression for heart failure." Dad looked up from the form toward me. "I have a pacemaker. I don't want chest compression. Chest compression would break my pace-maker. The pacemaker is expensive, so just let me die."

Stumped by my loss of words, I pondered how to ask Dad about the value of a pacemaker compared to his life. Unable to think beyond nice things, I never asked the right questions to get the correct answers. Instead, I said, "Dad, check the box for no chest compression." My reply seemed like a simple decision. I assumed he would suffer a heart attack at some time in the future and I would know exactly what to do. Our pacemaker conversation felt like a scene from a bad play, an unreal farce that I watched, something that wouldn't happen to me. I never asked Dad what he wanted if he was stricken with an embolism, kidney failure, and pneumonia.

"I need time to think and telephone my sister," I say to the doctor.

"I'll wait for your answer." He turns and walks down the hall.

In my call with Lauren, we remembered that Dad wanted a comfortable death. He didn't want to suffer.

I return to Dad's bedside. He chews on a corner of his blanket. Certainty of his end envelops me.

"I'm so cold," he murmurs.

"Goodbye, Dad." I tuck the blanket around his shoulders. "I'll miss you. I love you." I leave his room to answer the doctor's question.

Good Intentions

"Momma, why is Mable fat?" I shake my head.

"Let's see, Dicky." She lifts Mable from an oversized goldfish bowl that sits on the dining room hutch. Overnight, Jack Frost had visited our home to etch the dining room's French windows maybe in 1954; spring is still months away.

"Your pet Japanese-waltzing mouse is pregnant," Momma says.

I peer at the plump, black-and-white mouse that squirms and waves her head back-and-forth in Momma's hand. "What's pregnant?"

"Mable is going to have babies." Momma moves closer to me. "Look at the nest she built from cedar shavings to hide her young when they are born."

"When will her babies be born?" I gaze at the mound of aromatic cedar wood chips heaped on one side of the goldfish bowl.

"Soon." Momma returns Mable to her nest. "She probably became pregnant at the pet store before we brought her home. Now, run off to school. I'll put her bowl by the window

122

in a quiet place where she won't be disturbed. We'll check on Mable each day when we give her food and water."

One or two mornings later, I run to the kitchen. "Momma, Momma, let's check on Mable. I hear squeaks from her nest."

"Sure enough." Momma retrieves her finger from the bowel. "I count six babies. Baby mice are called pups."

I stand on a chair and watch blobs of pink, wiggling flesh, like the color of worms we use for fishing and about the size of brown beans Momma cooks for dinner. Cedar scent bathes my nose. "Wow, may I hold a pup?"

"Not now," Momma says. "We don't want to frighten Mable. She needs rest and quiet without distractions while she nurses her young. We want healthy babies. Get ready for school. You may check on Mable when you get home."

Later that day I climb on the chair to Mable's bowl. Instead of fragrant cedar, I smell a pungent odor like dead worms. I reach into her nest and touch wet and cold blobs of something that feels like raw hamburger. I jerk my finger from the bowl. Half-bodies, heads, and severed legs litter the nest.

"Momma!" I scream. I run to the kitchen to fall into her arms. "Somebody killed Mable's babies."

"Oh, dear Dicky." She wipes my tears and holds me to her heart. "I checked earlier. Mable killed her pups."

"Why?"

"Mable was probably a young mother. This litter could have been her first experience with babies. She may have been frightened and killed her pups to protect them from real or imagined danger. I intended to clean up her bowl before you came home. I'm sorry you had to see this."

"I didn't want the pups to die," I say.

"Of course not, Dicky. I'm sure Mable didn't want her pups to die either. We took good precautions with Mable, but death, like life, is unpredictable. No matter how well we plan, we are never ready for what happens."

∾

About fifty years later, I sit side by side with Mother in the dayroom at Oakwood Village, an assisted living community in Madison.

"He didn't want you—you know." She turns, takes my hand and looks at me. "What father wouldn't want such an adorable baby."

"I know." I sigh. I remember family photos where Dad held the infant, me, away from his chest as he might cuddle a porcupine in his arms. "I knew he loved me, he provided for all of us, but I never felt his love the way I wanted. Maybe he told me once that he loved me. Could we talk about something else?"

"Sure, what's on your mind?"

"I don't want to hurt your feelings, but I've been thinking—"

"About what, Dick?"

"Well, I think you'll be around for a while. Maybe it's time to make plans."

"What plans? Could you get to the point?"

"Your ashes," I say. "Where do you want me to spread your ashes?"

"Oh, yes. It's time. You haven't hurt my feelings. I want my remains cast over the spring where you placed Dad's ashes. Nothing special. Just make it nice."

"Are you sure? I understand why you want to be with Dad, but you never liked to fish with him at the spring. And what do you mean by nice? Do you want a ceremony or family to be present?"

"Yes, I'm sure about the location. Ceremony or family isn't necessary. Just say a few words, and let me be with Dad."

⌒⌣

In late spring or early summer 2005, I walk along the shoreline at the natural spring Mother requested to receive her remains. Sun reflects from the water's unbroken surface. Red-winged blackbirds chirp their seasonal welcome from bulrushes that circle the water's edge. My shoulder aches as I shift Mother's urn from left to right arm. Inside the container a twisted wire seals a gray-black mass in a plastic bag.

Her instructions were to cast her ashes over the water. Should I use my hand? I've never done this before. I open the bag to cast ashes directly as a farmer might broadcast a sack of seeds over furrowed ground. I swing the bag in an arc. Instead of lofting into air over water, ashes fall in a dark clump into the clear water. They settle on the buff-colored bottom.

I walk upstream for a fallen branch and return with a small limb. White paper birch bark shines in sunlight as I stir her remains to try to dissolve the ashes like brown sugar should disappear in cold water. Not much success. Dark remains turn to dingy gray as I continue to mix cloudy water. This, perhaps, is the best I will do.

I return to my car with the plastic bag and urn. A nearby sign reads: *No trash pick-up. Pack it in and pack it out.* I stow the plastic bag and urn and leave via an unpaved road, more bumps in my way as I head into town. At the high school's baseball diamond, I drop the bag into a trash barrel. Ashes spill from the bag.

"Darn, the bag's not empty," I mutter. A half cup remains in a fold of the bag. I don't want to leave her ashes in the trash, so I sprinkle them around home plate. Dark bone fragments contrast with white chalk used for baselines from yesterday's ballgame. I try to mix her ashes and chalk with the toe of my boot. Mother didn't like baseball, either.

Nothing Wrong with You

*L*et's assume today is a spring afternoon in 1954 or 1955. I sit near first base on the ball diamond at Maple Dale, my elementary school. I imagine this conversation:

"Dicky, are you crying?" A man's shadow moves beside me.

"No." I turn to see Coach Wagner.

"You sure look sad, alone on a sunny day." He sits beside me. "Something wrong?"

"No, nothing's wrong."

"You sure? I've known you since the day you were born. I know when you're upset. Remember when your father said you stole dimes from pocket money he left on his dresser? Your dad hurt your feelings, didn't he?"

"Yes, how do you know that?"

"You told him you borrowed Mercury dimes for your coin collection and intended to give them back. You were misunderstood. You felt bad then, just like now. So, tell me, what happened at baseball practice today?"

"It's my friends." I turn and look at Coach. "I'm always picked last. Neither side wants me on their team."

"Oh, I see. So, you think your friends don't like you?"

"I guess. Why else would I have to play right field? Nobody ever hits a ball to right field."

"Okay, I've noticed that you usually bat last. Is that your choice or your team's?"

"Pete says I have to bat last. He's captain of the Blue team, as you know. Same for Jimmy on the Red team. I want to bat first but I never get a chance because nobody likes me."

"Hmm, Dicky, please come with me to my office. I want to give you a test."

A few minutes later a white metal door closes silently behind us. The room smells of disinfectant. High on a shelf behind Coach Wagner's desk sits quart-size jar of iodine tablets. He distributes one pill to each pupil every Friday afternoon. I hate the taste of the tablets, but Momma says the medicine is for iodine deficiency, whatever that is.

"Please take this seat." He points to a chair at the back of the room. "Dicky, are you able to see the chart on the wall?"

"Do you mean the one with the big letter E?"

"Yes, could you read other letters below the letter E?"

"I see F and P on the next line and T O Z on the third line."

"Okay, please read the fourth line from the top."

"Coach, I don't see anything below T O Z."

"Dicky, I think you need glasses."

"Glasses? Why do I need glasses?"

"To see a fly ball, grounder, or a pitched ball when you're

at bat. I've noticed you miss easy catches in right field, and you take wild swings at home plate."

"I'm not good at baseball."

"I bet you could be very good at baseball, just like you are on the playground. You run well and have great stamina. It's just that you can't catch or hit a ball you don't see. When Pete and Jimmy pick their teams, they choose the best players. Both remember how many balls you've dropped, so they pick you last. If you could see the ball, you could catch or hit it. You need glasses. There's nothing wrong with you."

～

One month later, after baseball practice, I talk with Pete.

"Great double play, Dicky." He pats me on my back. "I'm glad I picked you for shortstop instead of right field."

"Thanks, Pete." I wipe sweat from my new glasses. "I was able to snag that hard grounder, tag the runner at second, and peg the final out at first base."

"Dicky, your double play won the game for the Blue team! I want you to bat cleanup at the next game. I'd like to see more homeruns, too."

～

Twenty or so years later, I stand in the corridor outside my instructor's office at the University of Wisconsin-Milwaukee. I'll call my professor Dr. Spencer. I imagine this happens:

"Oh, sorry," I say as my tortoise-frame glasses fly from my nose into a volcano of papers that erupt from Dr. Spencer's arms as our shoulders collide.

"Oh—Wilberg—not again." He kneels to gather his belongings. "Why don't you watch where you're headed?"

Watch? As Dr. Spencer closed his office door with an open book perched on top of his papers, he had stepped in front of me. Years later I would learn about the dangers of multi-tasking.

"At least you could help me find my glasses." On his knees, he runs his hands over disheveled papers in a blind search for his glasses.

"Here they are," he grumps. "Don't move. You'll crush my only pair." He snatches a pair of tortoise-frame glasses from behind him and squares them to his face. "Haven't you caused enough damage today? Now, if you'll excuse me, I have more important business than you." He squeezes between me and the wall and walks briskly down the hall.

Damage? Surely, he doesn't mean the question I asked at the end of his Astronomy 101 lecture earlier today.

"Dr. Spencer?" I had cleared my throat. "If Maarten Schmidt and Jesse Greenstein can't confirm quasars with red-shift theory, then how may they exist?"

"Rubbish!" Dr. Spencer had grabbed the lectern with both hands. "If you had carefully read your homework assignment you would have realized that quasars don't exist because they violate red-shift theory. That logic is the premise of my book."

Rubbish? Was Schmid's and Greenstein's discovery false? Eyeglasses lay on the floor behind me. Odd? How could my glasses have been knocked to my rear, opposite my direction of travel? I don the tortoise-shell frames, the bridge is a little tighter than usual, and lenses are slightly out of focus, but remarkably unbroken.

∾

Later that day…

"Hey, Richard, daydreaming again?" Pete grabs my arm. "Want to walk to the library to study?"

"Yeah, sure. I want to take another look at Dr. Spencer's book."

∾

Two days later, Dr. Spencer dashes to the front of the lecture hall. Chatter ceases when he clears his throat.

"I owe Mr. Wilberg an apology." He nods in my direction. Classmates' heads swing toward me. "I couldn't see Mr. Wilberg's point of view until after we collided in the hall. That night I reread Schmidt's and Greenstein's research. I saw things differently, a little blurry at first, but then I saw that quasars may exist if we accept the premise that fundamental laws of physics, such as red-shift theory, may have to be set aside to explain what can't be proven."

"And I too, sir," I say as I stand. "I'm afraid I judged your work from my personal perspective. After our collision, when I took a fresh look at your book, I was able to see your point of view."

"Now, Mr. Wilberg, please come to the front of the lecture hall." Heads swing back to Dr. Spencer. "I want to exchange your spectacles for mine."

Deception

*I*n 1954 the Village of Fox Point annexed portions of the unincorporated Town of Milwaukee, including my home, most of the neighborhood, and Maple Dale. On an overcast day, perhaps late that year at afternoon recess, a voice resounds across the snow-covered playground.

"Die, Nazi, die!" Schoolmate Gordon heaves an ice ball like an arrow into my friend Rudy. The ice ball slams into his shoulder. He spins backward and falls over the wall of a snow fort we had started to build. We call Gordon the Black Knight. His chest is like a barrel and hands are bigger than grapefruits. He shoots another snow arrow as I duck behind crumbled snow. Gordon has few friends and enough time to pack snowballs during morning recess, stockpile them in the sun to melt and refreeze in the shadows of afternoon recess to become arrows of ice.

"It's Gordon again, Dicky." Rudy crawls to my side. Tears frost his cheeks. "I wish he would leave me alone."

"Yeah, I know," I say. We became friends earlier this year. We sit next to each other in class because our first and last name initials are the same. Rudy's parents are second-generation German American. World War II is our passion. We play war games with pencil and paper every weekend afternoon. Rudy would draw an airplane with a swastika on the plane's tail. Then he would pass the paper to me, and I would sketch a tank with an American star on its side. Next, I would push the paper back to Rudy and he would draw lines of gunfire from a Nazi warplane that would strike the ground harmlessly around my American tank. Rudy would then return the paper to me, and I would draw tank fire to score critical hits on the enemy airplane. I penciled circles of smoke over the exploded aircraft and a spiral that tracked the doomed aircraft's crash to earth.

"You win, Dicky," Rudy would say. He always chose to be Germany. I never asked why.

Another ice arrow flies past my head. I pitch a snowball in return. Snow dust bursts harmlessly on the Black Knight's chest.

"Die, Nazi, die!" Gordon shoots an ice arrow into Rudy's leg.

I must save Rudy. I roll down the snow-covered hill toward the baseball diamond away from battle. The hill is pockmarked from boots of schoolmates, like crevasses on a mountain glacier that slow a mountaineer's descent. Ice arrows, like aircraft bullets that miss an American tank, fall around me.

I crawl to the backstop and run in a crouch toward the two-story, red-brick school building. At the front door, I sprint along a stand of Norway pines to circle behind Gordon. He doesn't hear my boots crunch on the hard-packed snow until he turns to see me grab his ammunition.

"Die, Nazi, die!" I shoot several ice arrows at Rudy.

"Hey, Dicky, here's more ammo." Gordon flips several ice balls toward me.

"Thanks, I'm tired of this." I point toward the pines. "Let's get Billy. He needs a face wash in the snow."

"Die, Billy, die!" Gordon lifts his snow-covered body and lumbers toward Billy.

∾

About fifty-eight years later, on a cool morning in late spring, Wayne and I walk from his house toward the barn. He promises to show me something special.

"*Killdeer—killdeer—killdeer!*" a bird's cry pierces the air. We step onto mottled, ashen-yellow-and-gray concrete pavement adjacent to the barn. With a hop and scuttle, a killdeer moves sideways away from our approach. She drags an extended wing behind her.

"Look," I whisper to Wayne. "She's injured."

"No, she's okay, Richard. She pretends to be hurt. We are near her nest. Unlike other birds that nest in trees, rock faces, barns, or other protected places, killdeer nest on the ground. Because of the vulnerability of their nests to predators, killdeer have mastered the art of deception, trickery similar to how a possum may pretend to be dead when a predator approaches. Many animals practice deception. Killdeer fake injury to appear vulnerable and easy prey. Let's look at her nest."

We walk toward the point of the killdeer's departure while she continues her charade.

A nest sits unprotected on the pavement. It includes several blades of withered, sun-bleached grass, a few pebbles, and cracked, buff-colored eggshells that match the color of the concrete pavement. Brothers and sisters wiggle and hunch lower in the nest as we take a closer look.

"What a terrible location for a nest," I say. "Why here?"

"Often, we don't see what's in plain sight. That's good. So, she chooses a vulnerable location. But if we discover her nest, and she perceives us as a threat to her young, then she will deceive us to move away from her nest."

Found Money

*E*nd of winter and early spring 1955 were the best times to find pennies, nickels, dimes, and quarters. Coins of these denominations and, sometimes in my childhood, half-dollars, would poke their formerly shiny faces, dulled by salt and deicers, from disappearing snow at the curb of streets. When crocus appeared in Momma's garden, pennies bloomed on Main Street.

Dropped from pockets, purses, and hands onto sidewalks, coins disappeared into snow and slush to await my discovery the next spring. Nickels, dimes, and quarters were most plentiful at bus stops and parking meters where commuters or motorists would remove gloves to search pockets and purses for money in the days before credit cards and bus passes. Coins slipped from Wisconsinites' cold-numbed hands to the accompaniment of colorful complaints.

Summer also yielded a plentiful supply of lost lucre, especially pennies. Most were pressed by automobile and truck tires into tar and gravel of the country road outside my boyhood home. A pocketknife could remove a recalcitrant penny when my fingernail failed. I dreamed of roads studded with pennies that shone like gold in afternoon light—my version of the yellow brick road.

In those days, I delivered morning newspapers by bicycle house to house. Each Saturday I visited customers to collect for my weekly deliveries, usually in coins. Lincoln wheat pennies, buffalo nickels, and Mercury dimes were most common. One morning, a man in a sleeveless white T-shirt smiled and handed me a penny. "This is your tip."

What is the value of a penny? Cumbersome in my pocket, they usually ended up in a pile on my bedroom dresser. Most people won't stop to stoop over and retrieve a penny from the sidewalk. Later in my life, I saw a man in Chicago move past a penny in a revolving door. When I stopped the door to retrieve my find, shoppers behind me shouted expletives.

Other people may intentionally discard pennies to lighten their load. I find more near high schools, where children could be careless, than around churches or at retail stores where pennies are offered in gratitude or sequestered in a dish near a cash register because a penny is still welcome.

Pennies used to have value at amusement parks to be crushed by a machine into a commemorative token as a reminder of your visit. My version of the amusement park-crushed penny was to place Abe Lincoln on a railroad track and retrieve the flattened, heated shim of copper after a freight train passed.

"Found money," Momma said later that year as she picked up a penny on the beach. Yes, definitely "found." If we defined the coin as "lost," we might be obligated to return the money to the owner. As a boy, I discovered pennies, nickels, and dimes too small in value for the effort required to find the owner. But when was the money I found not actually lost? If the intention of the person who let go of the coins was for the money to be found, then what they left wasn't lost.

∽

In 2001 or thereabout, I insulated the attic of our Madison home. Tongue-in-grove red pine floor planks were removed, each marked for correct reinstallation. I found a 1908 Indian head penny tucked between the rafters on a crossbeam. Did the coin fall from a worker's pocket in 1923 as he worked? Or did he choose to leave the penny to be found by someone in the future?

If the carpenter intended to leave the penny as a gift or as a commemorative token of his presence, similar to the penny transformed into a token at the amusement park, then the penny wasn't lost. Like an improvised time capsule, his commemoration was gifted to the future. I replaced the 1908 penny with a 1999 Washington quarter dollar and reset the attic floorboard.

Best Friend

*T*he rear tire of my bike leaves the paved oval track at Brown Deer Park on a summer day in 1955 or 1956. I skid. Uphill-bike pedal bites the asphalt. I spin. My knee scrapes asphalt, then elbow. My bike slides away. I stare at the sky. So far from home. Why did I ride here? No one to help. A voice calls my name. Maybe I'm not alone. I imagine Coach Wagner appearing.

"Dicky, are you crying?"

"Coach, why are you here? No, I'm not crying." Gingerly, I touch the angry red abrasion on my knee. "Dad says I'm too old to cry."

"Oh, I see." He squats nearby and sets a black athletic bag next to us. "I was out for a walk with my dog. I saw you fall and came over. Looks like you scraped your knee and elbow on the track."

"I don't see your dog."

"Oh, she's probably in the bushes on the lookout for rabbits. Would you like first aid for that burn?" He opens his bag. "I have Mercurochrome and bandages."

"Why do you carry first aid?" I wince as he applies the tincture.

"I'm a coach, and kids get hurt." He bandages my knee, then elbow. "How did you fall?"

"I tried to ride my bike on the track, and I fell. I'm so dumb. I can't do anything right."

"You're not dumb, Dicky. This track is a velodrome. Sides are sloped for high-speed bike racers. Do you know about centrifugal force?"

"I'm not sure."

"Centrifugal force pulls objects that move in a circle toward the outside of a circle, like bike racers in their lanes on these tracks are pulled outward and potentially off the top of the tracks. Racers lean into the slope to overcome centrifugal force. When you tried to ride your bike on the velodrome, you couldn't get enough speed to lean into the slope. You fell. Your bike slid to the bottom."

"Yes, that's what happened."

"You tried to do something that you had never done before. Don't blame yourself. Often, we don't know our limits. Come on, let's talk." Coach stands and offers me his hand. "I have a couple of bottles of red soda pop in the shade by that picnic table."

"My momma doesn't want me to have soda water." I take his hand, stand, and brush sand and dirt from my shorts.

"Oh, I think this time will be different." He leads me to a shady spot under an oak.

"Do you have a pet doggie, Dicky?" He hands me a cold soda pop.

"Yes. He's a dachshund, and his name is Hansie." I take a long, sweet drink of cherry comfort.

"What does Hansie like to do?"

"He jumps on the sofa and snuggles with us while we

watch TV. He also likes to sleep on Dad's bed. Every night when Dad wants Hansie to sleep on his rug in the kitchen, Dad yells, 'kitchen!' Hansie growls, jumps off where he is, and slowly walks to his bed."

"What else doesn't your doggie like to do besides bedtime in the kitchen?"

"He hates to be alone. One time while we were away, we had a thunderstorm. Hansie must have been frightened because when we returned, we found him stuck in one of the legs of Dad's pants that had dropped to the closet floor. He probably crawled into the pants because he smelled Dad. When we found him, Hansie was tightly packed and hot like a sausage. Maybe that's why dachshunds are called wiener dogs?"

"Ha, maybe." Coach wipes his forehead with a handkerchief. "What happened next?"

"Dad got a pair of scissors and cut his pants to get Hansie out." I laugh.

"Was your dad angry at doggie about his pants?"

"Nope."

"Were you mad because Hansie was dumb?'

"No, I love my doggie. He's my best friend."

"Dicky, could you love yourself despite the mistakes you've made, like you love Hansie? How could you be your best friend?"

PART THREE

Seeking My Truth

Muddy Middle

*F*ast forward to maybe1982. I sit on a lake-side bench on Navy Pier in Chicago. Morning sun hides behind clouds that hug Lake Michigan like the downy quilt that drapes my bed. I feel a presence behind me.

"Quite peaceful, isn't it, Richard."

"Coach Wagner." I turn. "What a surprise."

"May I join you?" He motions to an empty space beside me. "I assume you still call yourself, Richard."

"Actually, I'm not surprised to see you." I scoot over to make more room. "You seem to show up at the right moment and, yes, I'm still Richard."

"Good to see you." He runs fingers through longish-styled gray hair.

"You haven't aged at all," I say.

"I get regular exercise to stay fit. I'm here for a seminar. I decided to take a morning walk. I saw you and came over. What's on your mind, Richard?"

"Well, I don't believe you're here by accident, Coach. And I'm glad you found me. Like the last time, when we met at the record store, I lost my job. Actually, this time I quit and accepted another position at a company where I have little experience. My new job may also require more travel and time away from home, a big change for me."

"Yes, last time we discussed finding your authentic self. How are you feeling now?"

"I'm worried again and maybe feel lost."

"Understandable. Would you like some mentoring? I could share some thoughts and ask you to visualize an experience?"

"Sure, I could use your help."

"It's okay, Richard, to be unaware of where you are headed in your career or personal life. And not only is your lack of knowledge acceptable, to face an unknown like last time, it's desirable. Often, we jump from job to job merely to repeat what we've done before. Consider a walk in the wilderness, for example, where it's important to know your way. There may be dangers in the wilderness that could keep you from physically coming home. Short-term career or personal lack of knowledge of where you are headed, on the other hand, is an opportunity to discover what you want in work and life."

"That makes sense, especially about what I want." I reach for a cigarette but stop and return my empty hand to my lap. Coach might not appreciate my unhealthy habit; and do I really want a cigarette? More and more of my life seems like habits rather than actual choices. "But I'm uncomfortable when I feel lost. I want to be in control."

"Absolutely," he says. "Part of us always wants to be in control. But in reality, we control very little. And there are benefits in loss of control. Visualize feeling lost in your career or personal life as similar to being adrift in a sailboat on a featureless lake. No land is in sight nor wind to fill your sails to move you toward your destination, whatever that is. Water is the color of the gray, cloudy sky, a seamless blend with the horizon, similar to how Lake Michigan appears today. The lake bottom isn't visible, and the shoreline is unclear. You're in the muddy middle."

"Yes, that's exactly how I feel. What should I do?"

"Do nothing for now." Coach raises two fingers. "Like most people in a similar situation, you have two companions in your sailboat with you—your discomfort and your curiosity. To alleviate discomfort, most of us want an expert, a person with experience who will tell us what to do. We believe an expert may help. He has training in similar situations. We assume he will know what to do. An expert may be necessary in some circumstances. However, he is unlikely to have prior experience that perfectly matches your current needs. The expert may also be blinded by his own knowledge, with advice and recommendations based on his beliefs rather than what is right for you. And the expert may be in a trap of unawareness of what he doesn't know. Consult an expert, if necessary, but only after acknowledgment of your curiosity, the other person in your boat."

"So, maybe you're the expert?"

"Do you think so?" He smiles. "The expert tells. Do I?"

"Not really. You tell stories but never recommend what to do."

"Ha, you learn well. The other person in your boat is the curious you. Let's assume there is a curious person in all of us, and for simplicity, let's call this person her. When the expert gives advice, teaches, or recommends, he provides solutions. When the curious person self-reflects, however, she draws on inner knowledge, curiosity to understand current circumstances, and what brought her to this point. We wonder whether what we already know is true for ourselves and how to apply our self-knowledge to our current situation. When we self-reflect, we move out of our comfort zone, appreciate the value of the muddy middle, and become creative."

"I need a break," I say. "This is heavy stuff for early morning."

"I understand." He reaches in his jacket pocket, removes two boxes of grape juice, and two straws.

"Why did I know you'd have refreshments?" I open my juice box and begin to taste new understanding.

"We are creatures of consistency," he says. "Our brains are genetically wired to seek the status quo. When we are in the muddy middle, we have a challenge to move beyond what is normal for us, our comfort zone. Beyond our comfort zone we face change. Change implies potential danger because we are unaware of what we don't know."

"This sounds like my philosophy class in college."

"Indeed." Coach finishes his juice and puts the empty box in his pocket. "Let's return to our visualization of the unknowing place. Assume we are accustomed to a fast pace and are consistently aware of our destination. Our life is in balance. When we drift on our featureless lake, genetically derived danger signals flash. Our life is not in balance. We feel urgency to find direction. Our inability to see the bottom or the distant shore calls for action. In our near panic, any action will do."

"So, some of us may turn to diversions. Like substance abuse."

"Yes, or emotional responses, such as blame, anger, or any negative reaction." He removes a pencil from his shirt pocket and balances the pencil on his index finger. "Like this pencil, life seeks balance. Notice how the pencil teeters when I rotate my finger or touch the pencil outside of the balance point? Think of this example as your life. When the pencil is in balance, you are in your comfort zone. As I push down on the pencil away from the point of balance, the pencil may wobble and fall from my finger. I have awareness of how much pressure I can apply before I broach the tipping point."

"So, you say, when my life is in balance, and external events appear that disrupt this balance, like your finger on the pencil or being lost on a lake, I need to be aware of how much external pressure I can accommodate before I take action?"

"Right." He returns the pencil to his pocket. "When we grow our awareness in our ability to be uncomfortable and accommodate change, we feel confident beyond our comfort zone. When we accept our lack of knowledge about where we are or what will happen, we give up our need to be in control. When we are adrift on our featureless lake, we maximize our ability to find solutions that are appropriate for us. When we leave our comfort zone, we enter an area of lack of knowledge. At this edge of chaos, between what is known and unknown, maximum learning occurs."

"Like learning to ride a bike! I didn't learn to ride until I shouted to Dad to let go of my shoulder. That's when I left my comfort zone."

"Absolutely. Let go of your fears. Seek the edge of chaos when your vision is unclear. Stay as long as possible in the muddy middle. Be present with uncertainty. Avoid immediate action and, most importantly, skip the expert and trust your creative self."

Release Innate Creativity

*C*reativity may be learned. Edward De Bono in *Serious Creativity* (1992) defines creative as "bringing into being something which was not there before." Ken Robinson in *Out of Our Minds: Learning to be Creative* (2010) says, "Creativity is the process of having original ideas that have value."

Ancient Greek and Eastern cultures, on the other hand, believed the opposite. Creativity belonged to the gods. Human-produced poetry and works of art were seen as imitations of divine ideas. Renaissance poets and artists were thought to be divinely inspired. The notion that humans, beyond those who were gifted, could learn creativity as a process only emerged post-Enlightenment. And it was not until Graham Wallace's work in the early twentieth century that creativity was defined as a specific five-step process:

1. Preparation – scope
2. Incubation – subconscious
3. Intimation – hint
4. Illumination – consciousness
5. Verification – application

Hint is the germ of the idea, intuition that bridges subconscious with consciousness. If creativity could be practiced through a series of these steps, then giftedness is available to all of us.

We are creative beings, endowed with curiosity, passion, and mental capabilities to be creative. The design and function of our brain supports creativity. Information enters our brain from multiple sources and is stored in numerous locations. According to Robinson, when we recall from memory, information is combined with other data to create new patterns of thought. We remember very little, and our brain fills in the rest. Our minds are tasked with finding meaning. Our ability to innovate is a result of recombining information, most of which may not have been previously related.

In addition to our brain's search for meaning, we also see what we expect to see. According to David Eagleman in *The Brain: The Story of You* (2015), we are biased toward our beliefs and prior experiences. So, we visualize what we are conditioned to see. Think about visual puzzles, such as the profile of an older woman that becomes a young lady (see Steven Covey's illustration in *The 7 Habits of Highly Effective People* [2004]) or a duck that shape-shifts into a rabbit, among many other mind tricks. As these illustrations are turned or we change our perspective, the meaning in each illustration shifts. We're unable to see both females or the duck and the rabbit at the same time. Our brains pick one, then the other, one at a time. Our beliefs and prior experiences may prevent us from seeing multiple possibilities unless we are open to the possibility of multiple meanings in experiences as these examples show.

The greatest barrier to our creativity, however, may be

our perception of creativity. Just as we are endowed with creative minds, we are also hesitant to be creative. Robinson reports this paradox: "Most children think they're highly creative; most adults think they're not." He attributes this change in attitude to our culture and educational systems that teach conformity rather than innovation.

Reluctance to exercise our innate, creative talents is due to many factors. Chief among them are self-limiting beliefs, such as "I'm not creative," "I don't have time to be creative," or "I don't need or deserve creativity in my life." These types of thoughts deny us permission to explore our creative selves.

As a child I wanted to learn how to ride a bicycle. I don't remember having negative thoughts, such as "I'm incapable of learning how to ride," "I don't have time to learn," or "I don't really need or deserve to ride a bike." I do recall, however, having positive experiences. Dad bolted training wheels to both sides of the frame over the rear wheel of my bicycle to keep me upright as I learned. He ran beside me and shouted words of encouragement as I swerved from one side of the path to the other. Afternoons filled with practice included falls and ample Band-Aids to cover wounds prior to my first successful ride.

To learn to ride a bike is a good example of how to apply innate creativity to achieve something new. My experience may be summarized as including three conditions to release innate creativity.

Environment. Champions are necessary for creativity to flourish in your business and personal life. In the business world, champions include leaders who will run beside you and coach your creativity with words of encouragement. Company leadership may mistakenly establish creativity departments rather than mentor or coach creativity for all employees. Each employee is capable of creative thought. Champions in private life include your family and friends who will mentor and enable your potential. Find champions and gain their support.

Tools. Every trade or profession has tools for creative efforts. DeBono, for example, is a generalist on creativity and his tools are based on lateral thought. Traditional Western thought is linear, logical, and consistent. Lateral thought, on the other hand, interjects possibilities that are non-linear, illogical, and inconsistent, such as found in a joke. A joke is humorous because of the punch line that is related to the joke's linear story. Punch lines, however, are injected seemingly out of nowhere and therefore lateral to the logic of the joke's story. The surprise of the punch line creates humor. DeBono recommends tools to invoke lateral thought, such as mind maps, vision fans, and provocation. Use these types of training wheels or find tools for your trade, profession, or personal vision to use lateral thought to move corners in your life.

Practice. See the path ahead of you as you attempt to ride your creative idea. Talk about your idea, have a vision, and link your objective to your senses to put your intention into multiple locations in memory. When you grip the handlebars for your journey, feel the bumps in the path beneath you and experience the emotions of the moment. Find passion and excitement in the ride. Focus on the end of your journey as you swerve from side to side toward your ultimate destination.

Use your creative time in short bursts. Don't try to be

creative in one afternoon. Ride every day with frequent breaks to change your perspective and perception. It's important to get up from your desk, walk to the window for distant views, and reflect on your vision. Movement changes your mood and feeds creative energy.

Balance your life to stay upright on your chosen path. Maintain your social life, family, and friends to help when you fall. Accept failure as part of your experience. There are many Band-Aids in your box of learning. Use them. And when you are ready, remove your training wheels and ride to your joy of creation.

Three Steps for Creative Work

A photographer since childhood, I began with a Kodak Brownie box camera. Thank you Dad and Mr. Wagner for your support and guidance. In the late 1960s, I purchased my first professional film camera, a 35mm Nikkormat. A digital Nikon followed and eventually smartphone cameras.

Throughout my photography career I wanted to take better pictures. At some point I realized that when I take pictures, I photograph what I see without interpretation. I accept what I'm given. When I seek to improve my pictures, however, I change from a neutral observer of an event to an active participant. Now I understand that photography is an interactive process to *make* images with meaning. To do this I follow a three-step process of vision, composition, and pro-duction.

Vision is the essence of the photographer and the art of photography. Photography has potential to inspire. A visionary photographer is proactive. She selects objects to photograph to create meaning. A photographer who takes pictures or snapshots, however, is reactive, because she only captures information displayed in the viewfinder. A photographer with vision, therefore, interprets information and reveals truth when she makes an image. When truth is presented, a photograph provides meaning for a viewer. When a viewer is able to apply the truth of an image to the circumstances of his life, inspiration results.

Composition includes harmony of elements in a photograph. The primary element of composition is the subject of a photograph. Everything else is background. Background complements the subject. If the subject were removed, background must stand on its own. Subject is the focus of the photographer's vision, the main character of a story depicted in the image. When a photographer presents subject and story, she provides context and therefore relevance for viewers of the photo. Composition includes choices the photographer makes to communicate her vision. Vision is the essence of the photographer, and composition is the essence of the photograph. Vision is also the art of photography, and composition is the craft.

Production is manifestation of vision and composition for the viewer. The photographer produces her creation when she hangs her image in a gallery, publishes a book, or by any means reaches her audience. Where vision is the essence of the photographer and composition is the essence of the photograph, production is directed to the viewer. Unless you want to create photographs to please only yourself, the final test of production is usefulness or desirability of the photograph by others.

While the three-step process is applicable to improve photographs, the process may also be followed as a template for creative problem solving or innovation in other areas of our lives. Although steps may overlap, photography, and any creative work for that matter, may also be seen as a sequence of activities defined as before, during, and after.

Before we create solutions or innovate for opportunities, we start with vision, our ideas. Begin with assumptions related to your ideas. Do you take information about the situation and react? Or do you proactively seek alternatives and try to move corners? Recall that de Bono says the creative search for alternatives is lateral thought. One way to invoke lateral thought, he says, is through provocation. When we provoke, like the punch line of a joke, we think at right angles to linear thought. We consider illogical ideas. For example, if we want creative solutions to downtown parking, de Bono asks, "What if automobiles didn't have wheels?" Suddenly, a range of solutions appear, some feasible and some not.

During composition, we wonder, "What will be the impact of my vision on others?" We examine the context of our vision. We look at our idea as the subject of our composition as we would in photography and background as information. We consider whether elements of our composition (subject and background) are balanced and harmonious. We want to know if the truth of our vision will benefit others, and how will this truth be communicated. For example, let's assume you're a writer. When writers seek truth, they take information and make answers to benefit readers. They wonder, "What is the meaning of the situation I describe? Will the truth of my novel, poetry, or training manual provide help for readers?" Think of composition as development, testing, and application of prototype ideas during the creative process.

After the diligent work of vision and composition, production is the final arena for creative work. The focus of production is audience, customer, client, or any defined market. A measure of successful production is market acceptance. An example of disappointment in production of a creative vision and compelling composition is the failure of block chain technology and non-fungible tokens (NFTs) to deliver on promises. An older and probably more familiar production failure was the Edsel (Ford) automobile. If your product name becomes synonymous with "failure" or "lemon," as in the case of Edsel, you would have a classic production failure.

As you look at production of your vision and composition, ask, "Will my idea provide value and be accepted?" If your answer is less than a resounding "Yes," reexamine your vision and composition. Then make any necessary adjustments to production and finish your work.

Illuminate Ideas

*A*s a writer and musician, I want to create original content. I search for ideas to ignite my creative process. Other times I am blessed when inspiration materializes as I merely notice my presence in the world.

Beyond the farm lane, west of my boyhood home in rural Town of Milwaukee, prairie seemed to stretch beyond the horizon. Never mind that a hill blocked our views of Port Washington Road (U. S. Highway 141) and the rest of Milwaukee County. Perception created my reality, fortified when Dad joked that we could see Iowa on a clear day. On some overcast days, he became animated.

"Hey kids, there's a storm brewing!" he shouted as the screen door banged behind him.

My sister and I sprinted to the lane to watch clouds gather. Muffled thunder without lightning often announced weather's approach. Or bolts of light appeared before booms. Every storm was different. At this point in the storm's evolution, we'd dash for home and witness celestial drama from the safety of our garage. The storm peaked when lightning and thunder were simultaneous events.

Recall creativity previously described as a three-step

process for making photographs: vision, composition, and production. We logically think that ideas spark vision just as lightning illuminates the sky and precedes thunder. Creativity doesn't always begin with vision.

Steven Pressfield in *War of Art* (2002) and Elizabeth Gilbert in *Big Magic* (2015) postulate that an idea (vision) exists before we begin our creative work. They suggest that the next great novel or work of art already exists. Our job is to capture these distant ideas and make them our own. If we don't claim them for ourselves, others will.

On the other hand, John Dufresne in *The Lie That Tells a Truth* (2003) maintains that inspiration (vision) begins when writers write, not before we pick up our pens. When I want to write song lyrics (vision), for example, I begin with music (composition). From one's heart and soul, music is the source of feelings and emotions. I begin my creative process with music. Chords, melody, and rhythm become the ideas for my lyrics. Music writes the lyrics for me, my vision for the song. I use music to reach distant ideas within me, many are nonverbal, subconscious elements that are not accessible to my conscious mind.

Nancy Andreasen in *Secrets of the Creative Brain* (2004) speculates that Newton's idea of gravity did not occur when an apple fell from a tree and hit him on his head. The source for his idea, rather, resulted from twenty years of prior study of the universe. Similar to Newton, we may not have our discovery moment until years after we live with our vision. Then we are hit on the head and our idea seems to be a simultaneous flash of insight and explosion of action similar to the peak of a storm. That's when we know our idea was a result of our work instead of a flash of inspiration.

As previously discussed, Graham Wallas in *The Art of Thought* (1926) describes the moment of understanding as the point between our subconscious and consciousness when we have a "hint" of an idea. When we develop self-awareness to recognize hints, we are able to take action to move our hunches into words to manifest our vision.

Return to the storm. Distant muffled thunder hints of change in weather. We sense an emergence of an idea in the air. Some of us feel the change in our bones. At the peak of the storm, our vision is illuminated. Inspiration results from the storm. We manifest action and produce our idea.

Different Message

*I*n autumn of 1995, my future boss leans forward. With elbows on his executive desk, he dips his head. Over the top of his bifocals, he looks at me.

"Richard, I'm prepared to hire you to direct the development of our real estate, but there's one little problem."

"What's that, Kevin?" I fidget, lean back in my chair, and push back from his desk as if to gain distance from his problem.

"There are two Richards that already report to me. You would be the third." He reaches for his coffee mug. *Madison Mallards* is stenciled in gold letters above the team's logo. "Richard Webber goes by Richard, and his initials, RW, are the same as yours. And there's the other Richard with the same initials. I call him Rich. You'll have to change your name."

"Change my name!" I straighten my back. "What do you mean?"

"Not your last name." He leans back in his chair. "Just call yourself by a different first name. Maybe you could be Dick?"

Maybe I should have been Wesley after all.

∽

Over twenty years later, my music instructor for the prior three years, Nancy, picks up a pencil and draws a downward line that slopes across treble clef lines on a sheet of music notation paper.

"Music communicates in many ways, Richard," she says. "What if you compose a melody where your music goes down the scale from higher to lower notes?" She hands me her drawing. "In most of your songs, melodies ascend."

Later that evening I struggle to compose a melody that descends. Without a point of reference or awareness from an example, new music is difficult to create. I turn to Spotify on my phone. Soon, I hear a descending melody. I hadn't heard one until Nancy asked. When I paused and paid attention to what I needed, I raised my awareness, became present, and noticed what I needed to hear.

The next day I meet a client, whom I'll call Ben. We discuss his business brand, potential customers, and how he could increase sales.

"It seems like every time I meet a potential customer on her terms, I gain a new relationship," he observes. "Like, if I put aside my needs and listen deeply to her concerns, I increase my awareness of what she truly wants. Then, when I speak to her real issues, I make a connection, close a sale, and create a relationship."

On my way home, I reflect on Ben's insight. A descending melody plays on the radio. As I listen, I feel an awareness of a new level of communication the music has given me. Upon arrival at home, I get out of my car and walk up the path. A hawk, the medicine of fulfillment in some First Peoples cultures, flies across my path and perches on a tree limb about twenty feet ahead. I pause and gaze upward. Her eyes meet mine.

"*Owah*," she greets, not the typical call of "Kee-eeeee-arr" that I expect from a hawk.

"Yeah," I respond and continue to walk toward her.

"*Owah*," she replies.

"Yeah," I continue our conversation.

"*Owah*."

"Yeah." I stand directly beneath her. She turns her head, side to side, as if to get a better perspective of me, then wings away.

"I'm Hawk Talker," I shout.

A few years later, Wayne and I discuss my mother's legacy. I reach across his kitchen table for another glazed donut.

"I shouldn't, but may I?"

"Of course." He pushes a plate of sugar-coated delights to the center of the table. "Please do. I may have another myself a bit later."

"Mother collected rounded granite stones and nestled them in a basket like bird eggs in a nest." I wipe crumbs from the corner of my mouth. "Delicious. She collected weathered stones from Lake Michigan beaches, or river rocks as some call them, from streams or inland Wisconsin lakes. She preferred smooth stones, polished by water and sand into round or oval shapes. Some were red or brown-speckled, others were veined with contrasting igneous material that formed unusual patterns. Most were gray or off-white. Mother placed larger stones in a wicker basket, like kids use when they hunt for

Easter eggs. Smaller stones she tucked in a twig basket that resembled a bird's nest."

"Where did she keep these baskets?" Wayne reaches for a napkin and donut. "Later is now."

"She kept baskets in her dining room." I smile. "After she passed, we had an estate sale. The baskets weren't sold, so I consolidated all stones into one basket and brought them home—"

"And put them in your dining room." He laughs.

"No, I'm not sure where. Eventually they ended up outside in our flower bed. After a few years the baskets deteriorated, and the stones became two small piles. We added mulch to the flower bed and must have spread the stones when we raked leaves in the fall."

"Didn't you also have a landscaper to help you with your yard work?" Wayne reaches for a water pitcher and two glasses. "Cool drink?"

"Please." I reach for a glass. "Yes, the landscaper completed his work last fall. This spring when I raked, I discovered a patch of stones. As I picked them up, I was drawn to one gray stone in particular. I had almost overlooked this rock because most of the stone was buried. Too deep for my fingers, I grabbed a trowel, dug up the stone, and turned it over. Eureka!"

"What?"

"A perfect figure eight was formed by veins of a crystalline quartz-type of material in the oval-shaped, gray granite stone." I sigh. "At the same moment, a woodpecker began to drum in the nearby woods—"

"Do, do, do, do." Wayne hums the theme from the TV series, *Twilight Zone*. "I feel a twist in the works."

"Yup, woodpecker is a messenger, often from other dimensions, in some First Peoples beliefs. As I rotated the stone, my perspective changed. I received a new message. The figure eight became the symbol for infinity."

Change of Perspective

The Wisconsin River flows 420 miles from north central Wisconsin to the southwest to merge with the Mississippi River at Prairie du Chien, Wisconsin. At the river's mouth, he disgorges twelve thousand cubic feet of water per second, equivalent to the capacity of eight Olympic-size swimming pools every minute into the Mississippi. The Wisconsin River originates in pine forests and meanders through hardwoods, cities, farmlands, sandstone bluffs, and prairies before he reaches his destination. When we stand beside such a magnificent river and gaze at his turbulent flow, we assume what we witness today must have been similar in the past.

We are genetically conditioned to recognize patterns. We know other rivers and associate patterns of how those rivers flow to form our perceptions about the Wisconsin River. As a result of these assumptions, we fail to perceive evidence contrary to what we believe. We don't consider, therefore, the possibility that the Wisconsin River could have previously flowed in the opposite direction. We know water doesn't flow uphill and we have no reason to assume that the river could have flowed in the opposite direction. Therefore, we don't see proof that the river indeed flowed the other way millions of years ago.

Geologists have observed tributaries of the Wisconsin River that were not aligned to the river in the direction of the water's current flow. Normally, tributaries would intersect a river in the same direction as the water's movement. Scientists came to their conclusion about ancient river flow after studying aerial photographs. These views of the river elevated geologists' point of reference from ground level to a bird's-eye perspective. With this new point of view, scientists noticed tributaries were shaped like fishhooks where they intersected the river. This anomaly changed researchers' perceptions about the historic flow of the river and indicated that the Wisconsin River must have flowed in the other direction in the distant past. Although, such water movement would appear to be uphill today, the river earlier flowed downhill to the Lake Superior basin prior to formation of the Mississippi River.

Each day my creative work flows from origin to destination, similar to water in the Wisconsin River. When I write, sing, or compose music, for example, my perspective from where I sit limits my creative efforts. From a static location, my perceptions are linear and logical. I am blind to any evidence for new ideas for my work until I change my perspective. When I take a break, get up from my chair, and change my point of view (like the geologists did), I gain a different perspective.

John Dufresne (2003) urges writers to probe their subconscious mind. He describes the subconscious as our nonverbal mind and consciousness as our verbal realm. Since it is believed that the source for creativity resides in the non-verbal mind, he recommends writing prompts, brainstorming, free writing, and similar methods to reach our subconscious mind.

When we take a break from thinking, physically get out of our chair, move, and reposition ourselves in a different physical and mental state, our perspective changes. This shift in point of view enables change in our perception and ultimately may challenge our assumptions if we are able to see what we didn't notice before.

To change my perspective, I grab a smartphone and make photographs. I alter my physical location and mental awareness to allow a new perception. I'll let my camera show me what to photograph. Photographs reveal ideas for me. Since my images are unplanned (and therefore nonverbal) they enter my conscious mind from a subconscious place.

I don't choose subjects to photograph. That would be based on cognition. Instead, I let the objects of my photographs call to me. I'm often confused and wonder why I am drawn to photograph a particular subject. Upon later reflection, I often find meaning in an image. As a result, my perception of what I was previously working on shifts and opens new ideas.

Sometimes these ideas will not immediately materialize. Most of the time, however, new ideas emerge to guide my work. This change of perception—to see what I was blind to—provides inspiration for my writing, songs, and music.

Let's come full circle. When geologists elevated their perspective of the river, they altered their perception. With a new vision, scientists changed their beliefs about the historic direction of the river's flow. When we change our perspective, we are guided to examine our perceptions. With new vision, we may notice evidence of ideas that were previously unseen. When we acknowledge new information, our beliefs change, we move corners, and we take our creative work in a new direction.

What Do You Want
Me to Know?

"*D*ad, where's your mother buried?" I pull a side chair to his bedside in autumn or early winter 2003.

"Mother or stepmother?" He lifts his head from the pillow. His face is the color of the pale white bedsheet, draped like a shroud over his thin body. "Why do you ask, Dick?"

"Let me help." I reach to adjust his pillow. He struggles to sit up and lean against the bed frame. "Your mother, Meta," I say. "I never met her. You've told me stories, and we used to visit her grave. I feel I hardly know her. I might want to visit her when, well you know, when you're gone."

"Yeah, sure." He looks out the window beyond the beige walls of his bedroom at Oakwood Village, an assisted care facility in Madison. "My jail," he called his accommodations in prior conversations, but not today. Nor are dreams of one last trip to Texas or Alaska mentioned.

"Pinelawn Memorial Park in Milwaukee," he says. "She's buried in Section 12, way in the back, about twenty paces off the road under a big red oak—maybe two hundred years old. You'll find her there."

⁓

About nine years later—a cold November day it is. I enter the office at Pinelawn.

"Hi, my name is Richard Wilberg." I remove my gloves and shake hands with a man behind the counter. "I called for directions to find my grandmother's grave and was told to stop by your office."

"Of course, Mr. Wilberg. I'm here to help," he says. "Welcome to Pinelawn. Here's a map of burial plots. I marked your grandmother's grave on the map. We don't have gravestones, you know. We use plaques flush to the ground to mark locations. When you leave the office, take our driveway to Road H, then head to the left on Road M to Section 12. You'll find her grave at the far end, Plot 705, near the tree line. You won't miss it."

I take the driveway to what I assume to be Road H. Then make another assumption about Road M. Maybe I'll do better on foot, more able to see plot numbers. I walk parallel to graves to respect those who are buried. About fifty paces down the road, I turn at a right angle between plots.

An early winter wind hacks through the buttonholes and up the sleeves of my wool topcoat. Should I come back in spring? My resolve to visit the grandmother I never knew pushes me on. I reach the back of the cemetery as Dad said, near the tree line the man in the office described. No big oaks are anywhere to be seen. Maybe I'm in the wrong section? How would I know? I don't see any signs. Wind continues her pull, a test of my will.

"Meta, where are you?" I shout into the gale.

"*Rat-tat-tat*," a red-headed woodpecker pecks on a birch ten paces beyond where I stand. "*Rat-tat-tat.*"

"You're pecking on a birch, crazy bird," I yell. "Show me an oak."

"*Rat-tat-tat. Rat-tat-tat*," the messenger drums.

"Okay, okay, I hear you." My gaze drops to the toes of my shoes. I see the circumference of a dried oak stump, more than thirty inches in knurly diameter, cut flush with the earth, just below the top of the grass. I fall to my knees. Wind knifes my bare hands as I rub the bronze marker. I feel raised letters as if touching Grandmother herself. "Meta J. Wilberg," I read out loud. Dad never mentioned her middle name. I press my numb forefinger on the letter J. Energy of unknown words and emotions flow through me.

"Meta, Meta, tell me more. What do you want me to know?"

~

On one of our regularly scheduled days to write, Wayne and Nobu meet me at their door.

"Nobu doesn't like me." I sidestep the corgi's persistent lunge at my heels and ankles.

"Okay, Nobu, that's enough." Wayne waves a scolding finger as doggie retreats to the kitchen. "No, he likes you, Richard. Maybe it's your lamb's wool-lined slippers?"

"Could be." I begin to walk, and Nobu resumes his attack. "Whoa, boy. Corgis are bred to herd, aren't they?"

"Yup, but he's never seen a lamb in his life." Wayne laughs. "Dogs do what dogs do. He just wants you to know who he is."

Some months later, I eat a doughy and flavorless bagel in a dream. I toss and turn, then face brilliant morning sun. A corner of the bedsheet, crumpled and wet, hangs from my mouth and falls to the bed as bile climbs from my gut.

Another restless night, one of many since I visited Meta's grave. I remember my nearly fruitless search until that woodpecker (perhaps) guided me to her grave. The sharp, raised-bronze letters of her burial plaque that pressed into my cold numbed fingers, *Meta J. Wilberg*. J? Why didn't I know that? What else don't I know? And now the dream. What the hell does the dream want me to know?

I get out of bed, stuff my feet into slippers, and rub my neck. Coffee would help clear the frustrating dream and maybe a phone call to Wayne. He might help me sort out last night's dream and what he thought Meta wanted me to know. Oh boy, Meta's dead. How could she want me to know anything?

"Listening to ghosts now are you, Richard?" Wayne might ask. And I would likely reply, "Yeah, probably so. Sorry I brought it up." But no, not this time. Too many dreams and restless nights. I reach for my cellphone.

"Hey farmer, are you still asleep?" I laugh.

"What do you think, Richard. I've been up for hours. Got to get those cows out in the field."

"You don't have any cows. All you have is that slipper-eating Nobu. Could you be serious? I'm having a bad morning."

"What's up?"

"Remember when I drove to Milwaukee to look for my grandmother's grave?"

"Yeah, sure, shortly after your father died."

"I'm calling about last night's dream." I describe the dream. "What does it mean?"

"Wow, there's a lot here, Richard. I don't have an answer to your question about the dream, and I don't have any idea what Meta wants you to know. But I believe this. Stay with those questions. Be comfortable with ambiguity. Don't rush creativity. Some dreams may have a meaning. Others are merely practice for being present with your subconscious. And when you are ready to receive the woodpecker's message, you'll understand what Meta wants you to know."

I grab a pad of paper and begin to write a song.

Several years later, maybe 2015 or 2016, I stand in front of the stage at Crescendo Coffee and Music Café in Madison with singer-songwriter Mike Vial. Tonight Mike will debut my song Meta. I met Mike about a year earlier when he performed at another music venue in town. I liked his style, a hint of James Taylor that suited my song. I asked Mike to put music to my lyrics, the words my grandmother wanted me to know. A song birthed and a friendship created. I step on stage and grab the mic.

"I dedicate this song to my grandmother, Meta," I say. "I imagined my grandfather, a soldier in the German army over a hundred years ago, wrote a timeless message in a letter to Meta before he left for war. The message is what I believe Grandmother wanted to hear, not what Grandfather might have said. Meta channeled her message to me, and I wrote the song. Mike Vial will sing Grandfather's words as if

Grandmother was hearing his voice while she read his letter."
I introduce Mike.

He sings:

> META
> Meta, Meta. I love you.
> But I must leave today.
> Meta, I love you,
> More than words can ever say.
>
> Meta, Meta. I love you.
> I'll fight this war today.
> And I'll write you this letter,
> Before they take me away.
>
> I'll tell you I love you,
> The way that I want you.
> The way that I see you,
> The way that I need you.
>
> There's a knock upon the door,
> A fear I've never felt before.
> Meta, they're calling,
> I'll go, I must go.
>
> I'll soldier on alone,
> Though far away from home.
> The bugle that calls me,
> Will play your refrain.
>
> Remember I love you,
> The way that I want you.

The way that I see you,
The way that I need you.

Meta, Meta. I love you.
I must go on my way.
Meta, I love you,
More than words can ever say.

More than words can e'er express,
No poet can describe,
How I love you dear Meta,
My true heart abides.

How I love you dear Meta,
My true heart abides.

Until Now

One chilly morning in October or November, a woman briskly strides toward me. I stand on the abandoned, 36-hole, 400-acre golf course, part of Loon Lake Lodge. Could she be an employee of the bank? They foreclosed on the property ten months earlier. Or maybe she's a guest at the lodge like me? Sam, now deceased, used to invite guests, adjacent lakeside condo owners, and the general public to walk on his golf course when players were absent.

"Hi, gorgeous day," she says. "I'm Doris."

"Richard," I say. "Richard Wilberg, that is."

"Nice to meet you, Richard."

"Damn shame." I shake my head and gaze over her shoulder toward tufts of gray native grass that poke through formerly well-manicured, Bentgrass turf of fairway nine.

"We are close to winter," she says. "The land will look better in spring."

"Maybe." I sigh. "When the bank foreclosed, they discontinued maintenance. Lack of attention shows."

"Are you a golfer?"

"Nope. Dreams were lost as well as jobs for area families."

"The land will go back to the way it was. Not many jobs

were lost. People found other work. Are you from around here or a visitor?"

"I'm a guest at the lodge. Are you affiliated with the bank?"

"Nope. I'm the owner."

"I didn't know the property changed hands."

"This is private property, and you're trespassing."

"Well, I guess I should leave." I begin to walk, then turn back to face her. "I've stayed at the lodge for years. Off-season I'd walk on the golf course. I didn't know I was trespassing. Being unable to walk on the golf course is a real loss for me and probably others. Sam's death ended eighty years of family ownership. People worked, played, and died here. Sam's great-grandparents, grandparents, father, mother, and other family members are buried in a private cemetery in the woods between fairways one and two. Family pets also have graves there. I'll get along now."

A few minutes later, I return to the lodge. I find Sam's daughter, Christina, at work in the office with her baby daughter, Eloise, and young son, Justin. Christina is fourth-generation Smith family. But for Sam's death and the bank's foreclosure on Christmas Eve day, Justin and Eloise would have been the fifth-generation Smith family to own and manage the lodge and golf course. Christina wears jeans and a denim shirt appropriate for her working-owner role. She has operated the resort since her father's death. Her husband, Michael, works in town to help make ends meet.

"Hey, Richard, have a nice walk?" Christina hands me

a steaming cup of coffee. A blue silhouette of a loon under water with a fish in his bill is emblazoned on the white mug. I imagine Doris' face on the loon.

"Thanks for coffee." I remove my coat and sit at a table beneath a leaded-glass swag lamp, a common fixture in Northern Wisconsin resorts. "I met the new golf course owner. She wants to return the land to the way it was. I don't know what she means, and I'm not impressed with her hospitality."

"After the bank foreclosed, that same week on Friday, we found a buyer for our property who would allow us to keep the golf course." Christina joins me at the table. "Doris, however, swooped into the bank with her offer to purchase on Sunday before we could present our offer on Monday. What kind of a bank would make a deal on Sunday? Maybe that's why Doris won't speak with me?"

"I didn't know any of this," I say.

"How could you know? You arrived late last night. I didn't have time to warn you to stay off the golf course." Christina refills both mugs. "I'm frustrated with Doris. I sent an email to ask if we could walk on her property. She never replied. Five years ago, Dad sold her a lot for a summer home on the lake. She used to walk on the golf course when we owned the land. She never asked permission. I'm stung by the irony."

"Oh, man, that's tough."

"Yes. All I want is to take Justin for a walk on the golf course to the spooky woods, as he calls it. Justin often asks when we will see the scary tree roots that poke from the rocky hillside."

"I was headed in that direction when she confronted me. I remember those roots from last year. They looked like fingers that could snatch little boys who ventured into the woods. I also recall the bog past the trees—"

"Yes, one of many landforms created by the glacier that retreated ten thousand or more years ago," Christina says.

Years later, I will learn the glacier's official name is the Laurentide Ice Sheet. His snowy grip covered Canada with fingers of ice that grabbed North America as far as southern Wisconsin. Ice lifted a mile high over much of the state. The glacier gouged out basins for future lakes and depressed the North American continent. As the ice retreated, land rose without the weight. Scoured basins flooded with meltwater. Rivers eventually filled the future Loon Lake depression and the bog in the spooky woods.

"I love this land," Christina says. "When we designed the golf course, many boulders that the glacier left behind were too large to relocate. Some are the size of automobiles. We decided to let the big boulders, wetlands, and landforms determine the lay of the golf course."

"You also respected the land. You honored the natural features."

"We tried. I wonder if the period right after the glacier is the time Doris visualizes returning the land to? That was the era when First Peoples migrated to the region. These residents, known as the Woodland and Mississippian cultures, created effigy mounds that are still seen across Wisconsin."

"I studied First Peoples and effigy mounds in college," I say. Years later I will also learn that descendants of First Peoples are today's Huron, Menominee, and Anishinaabe (also known as Ojibwe or Chippewa). Ho-Chunk or Winnebago, as well as other tribes and bands, are also descendants. "First Peoples probably hunted and camped nearby and drank cool, clear water from the bog in the spooky woods."

"Yes, that's right. Or, maybe Doris thought of a million years before the glacier, when Lake Superior's depression was formed? Maybe she meant 4.5 billion years ago when volcanic basalt created the Precambrian Shield, the bedrock beneath all of us. I'm a geology major. I guess you can tell." She laughs.

"It's good to talk about this," Christina says. "In this general area, Precambrian Earth ultimately folded to create the world's third largest continental depression. The basin became an aquifer that later quenched the thirst of dinosaurs. Ultimately, glacial meltwater filled Lake Superior's basin, Loon Lake, and the bog in the spooky woods. Neither dinosaurs, First Peoples, native tribes, bands of today, Sam's guests, nor local residents needed permission to walk on the abandoned golf course—until now."

Everything Leads to Something

"*I* usually try to get to know my bosses' bosses," I say.

"Richard, do you mean one boss in particular or all bosses?" Wayne scoots his chair close to the kitchen table.

"How would you answer that question?" I smile and look at Wayne.

"I'd say you have someone in mind, but you used the plural of the object of your sentence and that suggests your statement also applies to all bosses." Wayne leans back and betters my smile. His hair curls from under his Wisconsin Badgers baseball cap, a constant fixture in his attire, even indoors.

"Astute," I say. "Yes, all bosses but one in particular. I remember how I met Tommy Thompson, but I've used a similar strategy with others."

"Governor Thompson?"

"Yup, none other. I was hired to develop an office park in Madison. Tommy's administration wanted to attract businesses to expand in Wisconsin. I preferred businesses to locate in my firm's project. I reasoned if I could meet Tommy and develop a personal relationship, I might have an edge with his staff and Forward Wisconsin. I'll get to Forward Wisconsin in a bit, but first, how I met Governor Thompson."

"You have my attention," Wayne says.

"Tommy had a speech scheduled at one of the downtown hotels," I say. "I don't remember the location. I thought he might leave by a back door rather than cross the ballroom floor and shake a bunch of hands. Sure enough, out the back door he comes, and I make an introduction. In the 1970s I met Mayor Maier of Milwaukee and in the 1980s Mayor Byrne of Chicago in a similar way. I know how to hang out around dumpsters. My strategy probably wouldn't work today with heightened attention to security."

"Cool!" Wayne chuckles. "Did your introduction lead to anything?"

"May I digress?"

"You usually do." Wayne laughs.

"Everything leads to something," I say. "I worked for C. W. Brubaker at Perkins & Will, architects in Chicago in the mid-1970s. Charles William Brubaker III, to be exact. He went by Bill. An executive of the firm, and an American Institute of Architects fellow, Bill mentored me. When a new opportunity emerged, Bill would often say, 'Everything leads to something.' I'm not sure of the origin of the phrase, perhaps Yogi Berra. On one business trip to Warsaw, Indiana, for example, Bill and I were seated on an elevated outdoor stage. We faced prominent members of the business community. Our sponsor, the president of the local bank, had just introduced us and as he returned to his seat, he walked past Bill, tripped and fell. Bill jumped up, and on live mic said, 'Oh, I'm sorry.' Everyone must have thought that Bill had tripped our host. We got the job to design the local library anyway."

"Okay, I get it," Wayne says. "A bias toward action, like the phrase 'any publicity is good publicity.' And similar to the quote attributed to Wayne Gretzky, 'You miss one hundred percent of the shots you don't take.' How does 'everything leads to something' relate to Tommy?"

"Like this," I say. "Bill would also say to me, 'Do something memorable.' Unfortunately, unlike the good outcome from the event on the stage, a memorable event might not achieve a positive result. I often expect an outcome based on what I want. I realize now that life isn't like that. I may influence a result, but I don't control the outcome. If I push one end of a cooked spaghetti noodle across my dinner plate, for example, I can't assume the pasta will go where I want. Similarly, if I count on a specific result from my interactions with people, I may be disappointed. Or worst case, if I try too hard to achieve a goal, move too fast, or I'm not clear with myself or others about what I want, I may receive something I never expected."

"I see where you may be headed with this story," Wayne says.

"Ah, yes, Tommy," I say. "I told my boss that I had met Governor Thompson. He thought my new connection would allow him to assign his responsibility with Forward Wisconsin to me. Forward Wisconsin is a public / private partnership of government and business leaders designed to facilitate economic development in Wisconsin. I worked with a savvy leader with good business sense who was a competent director at Forward Wisconsin. My assignment, along with a representative from Madison Gas and Electric, was to visit businesses in northern Illinois that are close to the state line. Real estate brokers provided us with a list of companies with less than two years left on their leases. We were to present opportunities for businesses to relocate to Wisconsin compared to Illinois. Benefits included lower business tax rates, reduced real estate property taxes if they chose to build, lower utility costs, better job training and schools, and substantial tax incentives."

"I've heard of those programs," Wayne says. "Some critics say incentives are abusive. They cost local government more in loss of taxes than the economic gains they produce."

"Yes, but in the 1990s incentives were moderate," I say. "Forward's efforts created some wins, enough to attract the attention of *The Chicago Tribune*, *Sun Times*, and other Illinois newspapers. They called us 'raiders.' Then the real fun began. Tommy erected billboards near the state line that said to motorists who entered Wisconsin that Wisconsin was a better place to live. Other billboards had similar messages, such as *Wouldn't you rather live here*, or *If you relocated your business to Wisconsin, you'd already be home*. Illinois' Governor Jim Thompson, known as Big Jim, reacted with billboards of his own that castigated Tommy's raiders."

"The border wars," Wayne says. "I remember."

"Any advertising is good advertising, I say. "Forward Wisconsin attracted many companies to Wisconsin. Big Jim reacted with more negative publicity that seemed to increase the exodus of Illinois businesses to Wisconsin. At the end of each successful year in Wisconsin, and there were many, Tommy invited Forward Wisconsin staff and volunteers to celebrate the year's work at the governor's mansion on Lake Mendota. Although I was part of Wisconsin's success, none of the firms attracted to Wisconsin selected my firm's office park for their new location. I knew I had to get more personal with Tommy."

"This is a long story, Richard," Wayne says. "I have a hunch you'll do something memorable."

"Almost." I sigh. "Remember my Harley Sportster?"

"Yeah, I think so."

"I had a Norton Scrambler before I bought the Harley. The Norton was notoriously unreliable. When I took a trip, I had to be sure no rain was forecast. If I got caught in rain, I couldn't start the engine. I was stranded many times, so I bought what I thought was a more reliable Harley Davidson Sportster. Unfortunately, the bike, although reliable, had an uncomfortable seat with handlebars that vibrated, making my teeth chatter, resulting in headaches. Sportsters are small, powerful, city bikes not suitable for long trips.

"Tommy rode a Harley, too. He favored a big over-the-road classic model, a sofa on wheels with saddlebags, leather fringe, and chrome trim. Each year Tommy would round-up a bunch of business executives who owned Harleys and they would motorcycle to Washington, D.C., to present business issues to Congress and President Bush.

"Over the years, I got to know Tommy better when we talked about our Harley connection. I must have inflated my motorcycle ability and the capabilities of my bike because at the last party I attended, Tommy shouted to his assistant, 'Add Richard to the Washington trip list.'"

"How great." Wayne beams.

"Not really." I sigh. "When I heard Tommy, my face flushed, and my hands went cold. I could hardly ride from Madison to Milwaukee without a visit to my dentist. How could I motorcycle a thousand miles to Washington, D.C.? But, more importantly, how could I turn Tommy down?"

"So, what did you do?"

"The only thing I could do. I said, 'Sorry, Tommy, I have other plans.'"

When Is Enough?

I imagine Pete and I sitting in a coffee shop in Green Bay, Wisconsin, and having this conversation:

"I never want to stop," I say. "Maybe I've started to write a song for piano composition on the back of a napkin. Eventually, I'll run out of room, or I'll start to make changes and begin to lose the idea that started my work."

"Richard, you've described what happens when I write an essay," Pete says. "My writing coach advises me to continue to write. Save the edits for later. Writing is right brain, a creative activity. Editing may be creative, but revisions are left brain, linear, and functional."

"That makes sense," I say. "I use abbreviated jazz notation in alphabetical letters to transcribe left-hand bass chords and right-hand melody notes. When I go back to the piano a day later, I have difficulty remembering the details of my initial composition. I don't remember nuances such as whether the music goes up the scale or down, so I record the melody on my phone."

"I do something similar," Pete says. "I make margin notes or highlight text to come back to later. Or I may write paragraphs, not in the order of the story before me. I may use these snippets in the essay I'm composing or save them for another project. The point is to keep writing."

"I use riffs in my music, similar to your snippets. I don't use music notation software, that seems too left brain for me. I transcribe my riffs in standard notation, using old fashion lined-bass-and-treble-clef music note paper."

"You're so 1970s, Richard!"

"I know. A number two Ticonderoga pencil and a Pink Pearl eraser, worn to an oblong like a miniature football burnished with graphite, get the job done."

"After business school," Pete says, "I crunched numbers on real estate proformas on computer spreadsheets for real estate developers. Do you remember the expression GIGO?"

"Sure do. Garbage in, garbage out."

"I feel the same way when I write an essay," Pete says. "I have friends who use pencil and paper. They don't want a computer between them and their creativity. If I'm going to produce garbage, I want to know its garbage, not the some-what-intelligence of a machine to decide for me."

"Did you take typing in high school?" I ask. "I realize I'm somewhat off subject here, but bear with me. I took typing so that I could type my term papers for college. I didn't want to hire a typist. That fluke of a decision prepared me for an easy transition to personal computers later in life. The downside is I'm tempted to use my computer instead of the piano."

"I didn't take typing in high school," Pete says. "Wish I had. I have to hunt and peck on my computer. And I totally get why you don't want to use music notation software or commit your music to standard notation too soon. When I separate myself from the creative phase of my work with editing on a computer before I'm ready, I put a premature end to my essay."

"Let's take a walk," I say.

Afternoon sun warms my face as the slanting rays promise a change of season. We wander along a well-trod path through a local park. Like my creative work, I've followed familiar pathways many times.

"I get your dilemma," Pete says. "When is enough?"

"You got it, Pete. I have to commit riffs to standard notation in a somewhat final format for my piano instructor to follow my progress and guide my work. I also want to get to a point where I'm beyond my draft and reliance on my memory for details. You know what?"

He shakes his head.

"As soon as I commit to standard notation, I begin to make changes. My work keeps growing like a flower in a root-bound pot that searches for space to grow."

"Like our lives, Richard. We are enough—for now."

Tom's Crow

"*M*aw, maw." My neighbor, Tom, has a pet crow that caws above the din of his portable radio tuned to 1950s top forty hits. I'm painting my home in Madison on a summer weekend. I lean back on my ladder for a better view of the source of the racket.

"Good morning, Richard." Tom waves as he moves the crow's portable perch to a shady spot on his deck. Similar to a wood clothes rack for hats and clothing but without hooks, the device includes a dowel for a crow to perch. In pleasant weather, the crow's rack and radio appear on Tom's deck.

"Morning, Tom," I say. "Beautiful day."

"What's that?" Tom lowers the radio's volume.

I wave and continue to paint. He returns the radio's volume to high. Tom selects the same AM radio station to share his favorite music with neighbors. Radio volume, like the crow's caw, is always set too high. Today, the crow competes with Fats Domino's musical memories.

"*Maw, maw*." The crow prunes his feathers and lifts his left leg to scratch his breast.

"Enough!" Tom slams today's *Wisconsin State Journal* on

190

a deck table. Coffee spills from an overturned cup. "Now see what you've done."

"*Maw, maw.*" The crow continues to scratch.

Enough indeed. I climb down the ladder and stride through Tom's gate into his backyard.

The crow or the radio has to go. What shall I say to Tom? I want peaceful days in my backyard and good relations with my neighbor.

"I found my thrill, on blueberry hill," Fats croons.

"*Maw, maw.*" The crow accompanies Fats' lyrics.

"I know," Tom says. "He drives me crazy, too. I've decided to take the crow for a ride to the country."

"Where did you get the crow?"

"After a storm earlier this year, we found him on the driveway. He must have been washed out of his nest. We thought our rescue of a baby crow was the right thing to do. We named him Oscar. Each day Oscar would caw when Ellen approached to feed him."

"Maw, maw," Oscar replies to the mention of Ellen's name.

"Yes, I know," Tom says. "Ma will be home soon. At first, we thought Oscar's response to Ellen's appearance was cute. We never realized Oscar would continue to chatter as he grew older." Tom waves to Ellen as she drives her car toward their garage.

"*Maw, maw.*" Oscar turns on his perch to watch Ellen's car.

"Sunday I'll drive Oscar to Middleton. There's a wooded area next to an office building on Parmenter Street about a fifteen-minute drive from here. I'll release him in the parking lot."

"That's great, Tom," I say. I wish he would also take Fats Domino on the ride.

"Hi, guys, how's your morning?" Ellen skips up the steps to the deck. Oscar watches in silence.

○

For the next three weekends, I enjoy the relative quiet of Tom's AM radio sans Oscar's accompaniment. Then, on the fourth Saturday after I first met Oscar, I enter my backyard to a familiar refrain.

"*Maw, maw,*" a crow caws.

"What's going on, Tom?" I lean over the fence and gesture toward the crow rack. "Is that Oscar?"

"He showed up last night. My daughter's car broke down, so she borrowed Ellen's to drive to work. Emma works at a dentist's office next to the woods where I released Oscar. At the end of the day, when Emma left work to return Ellen's car, Oscar followed her all the way back here."

"*Maw, maw,*" Oscar proclaims, while on the radio Danny and the Juniors scream, "Let's go to the hop (Oh baby)."

Trust Self-Knowledge

*W*aves rippled in Kodak Dektol developer each time I plunged my warm hand into the 68-degree fluid to process photographic prints. Prior to digital cameras, photographers could send negatives to labs to make photographs or develop their own prints. I chose my basement darkroom to produce pictures to find personal truth within my photographs.

I used tongs and other darkroom tools to place image-exposed Kodak Polycontrast paper into developer fluid. Agitation of the paper by shuffling it back and forth removed air bubbles from the paper's surface. Free of bubbles, Dektol could uniformly penetrate to the embedded silver within the paper to create the image I wanted. I used my hand to agitate the paper. In spite of the cold, I enjoyed the tactile sensation as I moved the paper forward and backward in the fluid as if to coax the image to come into view.

At first, a ghostly vision appeared on the paper's surface. Removal of the paper from the developer at this point would produce an underexposed image without detail. To keep the paper in the developer too long would produce an equally disastrous result. Overexposure would hide the photograph's story in a dark mishmash of excessive detail.

Why is discernment critical, you might ask? When the image is ready, why not remove the print from the developer? Unfortunately, photographs continue to develop after the paper is removed from Dektol and placed in the fixer, the second step in the process. Discernment, based on self-knowledge from prior experience in the darkroom, told me when I should fix the image.

To rely on self-knowledge requires trust that what we know from the past will be useful in the present moment. Sometimes we may want more information to confirm our instincts. Often the information we believe we need to confirm self-knowledge may overdevelop our vision and block our truth, similar to the overdeveloped print in Dektol. How do we trust self-knowledge to find the optimal point to stop developing our vision and move forward? Look to the seashore as an example.

We know the ocean will continuously deliver waves to the beach as she has for millennia. Just like we trust the sun to rise in the morning, we have faith in the natural rhythm of the ocean. Does the sea metaphorically search for information on how to produce each new wave? Or does her self-knowledge, born of tidal and geologic forces, allow her to create waves without deliberation? Obviously, the latter.

The sea has her own version of self-knowledge. Not a mental capacity but an energy linked to natural forces, geologic patterns, and tidal energies that shape the repetition of waves, each meeting the beach before an earlier wave fully retreats. The ocean knows, in an energy sense, the optimal time to release each new wave without information about the return of the previous wave. The overlapping, foamy intervals flow forward and backward, as if processing the sea's truth in Dektol.

Each wave is evidence of the ocean's self-knowledge of how to make waves. The ocean doesn't seek confirmation of her ability to produce waves. Nor does she need to see the result of each wave prior to creation of the next. No one questions her ability to make waves or the validity of the ocean's purpose. We accept her natural knowledge and behavior as the essence of an ocean.

How could you use self-knowledge as your essence? Would faith in your discernment to cease development of your vision at the optimal time achieve your truth? Your truth, like the print in Dektol, is what's meaningful to you. You don't need every fact to fix your image, nor do you continuously need more information to reach your goal. You also don't need confirmation of your ability. Trust your capabilities and the natural rise of self-knowledge as the wave metaphorically trusts the ocean. You'll know when it's time to stop development of your idea and create the vision of your truth if you trust self-knowledge.

Listen to Be Present

*T*o be present with others is an important requirement of successful relationships. We build relationships through meaningful conversation. Susan Scott in *Fierce Conversations* (2004) says, "Conversation is the relationship."

When we are present in conversation, we are in the moment with our attention toward the other person. When we are present in meaningful conversation, we do not check our phone, think of what we will say next, let our attention drift, or have thoughts about ourselves.

To be present in conversation is to listen in order to understand. Marcia Reynolds in *The Discomfort Zone* (2014) suggests "three centers of knowing" for meaningful conversation. We listen from our head, heart, and gut to capture meaning.

When we listen from our head, we hear literal meanings of spoken words. We "head listen" at a rational level to solve problems in cognition together.

When we listen from our heart, we sense high order emotions, such as sorrow or regret. We recognize emotion in the words and see the body language of the other person. When we "heart listen," we empathize with the other in what we hear and see. We heart listen to relate with the other person at a deeper level.

When we listen from our gut, we intuit emotions or other states of being that may not be evident in the conversation. When we "gut listen," we search for meaning beyond our head and heart. We may sense base-level emotions, such as fear or confusion. Gut level emotions are survival instincts. Thomas Lewis in *A General Theory of Love* (2001) describes gut feelings as "reptilian." We gut listen to relate to the other person from a primal state, the deepest of the three levels.

To simultaneously listen at all three levels in a conversation is similar to how we listen to a song. Think of how we head listen to lyrics, heart listen to melody, and gut listen to instrumentation.

Lyrics tell the story of the song. Words of the song may include techniques such as rhyme and repetition to reinforce the listener's attention. Lyrics are primarily created in the left hemisphere of the brain, our logical mind. To hear lyrics, we head listen. When we listen to the other person from our head, we hear her descriptions. We listen for logic, the rhyme of her tale. We listen for reasoning, through the repetition in her words. We hear what she believes.

Melody is the song's tune, the arrangement of notes and voice to reach our hearts. Melody and vocals carry the song's meaning and may be supported by chords and other note arrangements to achieve the composer's intention. We relate to melody and vocals when we say, "A song touches me." We may describe vocals with a metaphor, such as "the voices of angels." Metaphor is right brain abstract thought, the property of the heart. We heart listen for meaning beyond words, the chords that reveal the truth in her story. We listen for unspoken words, the silence between the notes that gives a deeper message, and the emotion in her voice.

Instrumentation supports melody and vocals at heart and gut levels. When we listen to a bugle play our national anthem, for example, we hear with heart. "My chest bursts with pride." Now think of percussion that expresses the rhythm of the song. Ancient cultures used drums to rally warriors, reaching gut level emotions of fear and bravery. We gut listen for intrinsic emotions, the beat of the drums that accompany her words. We listen for urgency of sound, or calmness, and the rhythm of her voice and body.

Singer-songwriter Jimmy Webb in *Tunesmith – Inside the Art of Songwriting* (1999) says, "A song is a magical marriage between a lyric (some words) and a melody (some notes). It is not a poem. It is not music. It is in this gray area of synthesis of language, rhythm, and sound that some of the most acute of all sensors of human emotions lie."

In your next conversation, could you open gray areas as you tune in to your sensors of human emotions? What would it take to listen at all three levels for meaningful conversation to strengthen your relationship? Could you listen to be present and understand?

I'm Here for You

To recognize when we are judgmental is crucial for meaningful personal and business conversations. When we judge, we conclude based on self-talk that includes our beliefs, assumptions, and prior thoughts. We don't hear the words, nor do we sense the body language of the other person in our conversation. When we are judgmental, we are not present. To have productive conversations requires that we recognize our potential judgmental tendencies.

To be judgmental and to exercise judgment are not the same. When we practice judgment, we discern alternatives. We discern every day, for example, when we choose our food for lunch or decide what clothing to wear or make any other choice based on objective information.

Being judgmental, on the other hand, is a subjective act. Judgment kills dynamic conversation. We may realize a subjective mistake after a failed conversation when we receive feedback or upon self-reflection. But how do we recognize if we are judging while we are in a conversation? And if we identify any detrimental role in our discourse, how do we take corrective action?

Let's start with the relationship between knowledge and behavior. We may know behaviors to avoid, such as excessive speed in our automobile. We may fail to recognize, however, when we exceed the speed limit unless we pay attention to the speedometer. Our speedometer is external assistance for awareness to facilitate corrective action, as in this example, to reduce our speed.

Sometimes what is required between knowledge and corrective action is internal awareness. Can you remember a time when you were in a group discussion and the facilitator, or worse yet your boss, asked a question? Silence filled the room until one of your peers responded. You may have thought, "I knew that." But you failed to answer. Your lack of response may have been due to fear of being wrong, or because you could be an introvert, or any other personal reason. Or you did not recognize you knew the answer; you lacked awareness so you failed to respond.

You might have thought, "I had a gut feeling about that." Your feeling could have been intuition, your internal assistance for awareness. Until you move intuition into consciousness and take action, you will practice knowing without doing. So, how do we know when we are judgmental or when we are on the path to be judgmental? And, most importantly, how do we move our knowledge into corrective action when we are or will be judgmental?

Like the automobile example described above, I use road signs to warn me when I'm in judgment or will be judgmental. To know these signs allows me to watch for judgmental behavior and to take corrective action if I have judged. Just as we check our speedometer or traffic control signs on the highway to adjust our speed, we do gut checks to test intuition, I watch for six signs when I could be tempted to judge or when I'm already in active judgment. Let's assume you are in a conversation with me, and I recognize one or more of these six signs in me.

Labeling a person or event. If I label, or respond with an opinion, I arrive at a conclusion based on my beliefs rather than what you said. I have voided your words and won't meet your need to be understood.

Drifting away from conversation. If my mind wanders, I'm not attentive to what you said. If I'm not attentive, I have not listened. If I have not listened, I'm not in true conversation.

Impatience or emotional disconnection. If I'm impatient, I've shifted from you to me. I have focused on my emotions rather than your words and feelings. And if I've experienced an emotion that is inappropriate for what you've said, I've disconnected from the conversation. If I become angry as I listen to your happy story, for example, something has been triggered within me. If I recognize my emotional disconnection, I may refocus on the conversation and what you need.

Breached Values. If my values are tested in a conversation, my objectivity maybe compromised. Values reside at the core of our existence. Although I may believe I'm objective when my values are tested, I need to examine how I will respond. Will I act based on what I treasure or in accord with what is appropriate for you? This question is a test of my objectivity.

Sympathy and taking sides. Sympathy is usually thought of as support. However, if I say, "Oh, I'm sorry," I have shifted to my feelings and away from yours. Or if I say, "How could he do that?" I've entered your story and have taken sides. I'm no longer objective. If I show empathy, on the other hand, I hold you in first place. If I say, "What do you need?" I've focused on you rather than your story. Or if I simply remain silent and maintain my presence, I've held you with empathy. Empathy is the best support.

Shifting to solutions too soon. This road sign is a trap, especially for someone like me who wants to help. When I prematurely move toward solutions, I have undermined your thought process. I've switched from being a listener to *doing* repair. And maybe you don't want solutions, you just want to be heard. If solutions are indeed what you're after, they will arrive in their own order. All I need to do is shut up, listen, remain silent, and wait. Then I will mirror Thich Nhat Hanh's eloquent words with my presence: "Darling, I'm here for you."

Repair My Divots

I'm an average golfer, and I see golf as more than a game. Therefore, being average is okay.

In my youth, I learned to play golf with my father's hand-me-down clubs. Dad bought left-handed sticks, as he called them, so he gifted me his right-handed Ben Hogan woods and Sammy Snead irons. A southpaw in most areas of his life, he may have thought right-handed golf clubs were the reason for his poor performance on the links. We never played together, so I'm unsure if his game improved with new left-handed sticks.

To learn to play with left-handed clubs must have been a challenge. I assume Dad immediately changed from right to left. How does one swing a baseball bat, tennis racket, or golf club, for example, to the right on Tuesday and switch to the left on Wednesday?

I learned French in high school. I didn't stop conversations in English and completely change to French. I spoke both languages and relied on English as I learned French. Dad went cold turkey on right-handed clubs when he adopted left clubs. He couldn't use both sets of clubs the same way I learned French. I never asked how he made the change. I had challenges of my own.

Two inches taller than Dad, I found my hand-me-down clubs to be too short. I had to hunch over the ball. This posture seemed okay because if Dad could learn to swing left without a smooth transition from right, I reasoned that I could accommodate my own variation of difficulties. We both had problems to overcome.

I spent little time on the golf course due to inadequate equipment and low motivation to improve my game. As a project manager in business, I spent most of my golf career involved in charity golf events with clients in which individual performance wasn't important. In charity golf, also known as best ball, a foursome tees off. Then the group checks the lie of each of the four shots relative to the green and chooses one ball to play. Players alternate shots with the best ball until the ball drops into the cup on the green. As a result of best ball, and my ball usually wasn't best, my game didn't improve. For the same reasons, I learned about divots.

Divots are small chunks of turf players slice from the fairway when they cut the club too deeply under the ball, often to send the turf further down the fairway than the ball—quite an embarrassment. Divots may occur anywhere on the fairway but typically happen closer to the green. Here, a golfer selects a club, usually an iron, more like a shovel than a fairway wood, to get under the ball and lift the ball to drop close to the cup. Loft of the ball to stay on the green is the objective. As a result of my short clubs and amateur ability, I created many divots and became knowledgeable about the importance of divot repair.

I learned how to interrupt my game, walk forward to

the divot, pick up the limp fragment of soggy sod and walk back to the wound I had created in the fairway. Then I would replace the displaced turf by tamping it down with my foot. I also understood that replacement of divots must be done quickly because turf will dry out. Lack of moisture hampers a divot's repair. And, when possible, the divot should receive follow-up attention by grounds crew to water and give nutrients to guarantee success of the regrown grass. Divot repair is important because restoration of the fairway to the pristine condition that existed prior to the divot benefits other golfers. Timely care keeps the fairway smooth for everyone's enjoyment.

Although it's a simple act of courtesy, I notice many golfers don't replace divots. Why? To replace a divot takes time. When golfers are close to the pin, called the short game, they focus on how to finish the hole. Divot replacement may be thought of as a diversion from the game. Replacement takes time and effort. A golfer that makes a divot must move backward, and golf is about forward motion. Handling possible wet and muddy turf may be messy. And the foursome behind yours could be annoyed when their game is delayed. Furthermore, the golfer who makes a divot may believe that no one noticed so why draw attention to his mistake?

Divot replacement and repair provided me with practical education on the importance of repair of social or business mistakes. In my career, I often asked associates who were avid golfers, "Where else don't you replace divots in your work?" Associates pondered how often they had failed to take time to heal a social or business wound.

Repair of social or business transgressions is critically important. I start with the assumption that someone noticed my social divot. There aren't trees in the office, like on the fairway, to hide my mistakes. Also different from the links, businesspeople are paid to pay attention. Careers benefit from critical observation. And, most importantly, repair of social relationships is the right thing to do because timely repair of my mistakes allows me to move forward as a player in the business game without adopting defensive energy. Others who play beside me in a business relationship will benefit from my attention to the repair of rough surfaces in their paths.

So, when I realized how I had interrupted an associate, whom I'll call Mary, while she spoke at a staff meeting, repair of my transgression required timely action. Rather than delaying an apology, action now would benefit both of us. When I stop my current activity (my short game) and walk backward in time to Mary's office, I will attend to her hurt feelings. If I'm able to see her and replace my divot, I will heal Mary's wound with my watering of apology and attention. Yes, my repair may be messy, and I may feel uncomfortable. But when I recognize how short-term actions may improve my relationship with her, I will practice desirable leadership behavior for myself and for her, and I will act as a role model for others.

Thistle Seeds on the Wind

I'm a starter. When I read, I place a bookmark where I've left off. I intend to finish later. Sometimes I do. Often, not. Bookmarks wag from unfinished volumes, stacked on top of my bookcase, like multiple versions of my first grade teacher's tongue.

"Tsk, tsk, Dicky," she admonished. "Put some ethyl in your tank."

I wish I had my current wisdom back then to tell Mrs. Higgins, "I love the rush of new ideas. My work will be completed in its own time."

Why are we excited about new starts? When we begin projects, we give ourselves permission to make mistakes. Writers are encouraged, for example, to get thoughts onto paper or digital media to create a "shitty first draft" as Anne Lamott suggests in *Bird by Bird* (1994). Revisions, the real work of writing, will follow in due course. With each subsequent draft, our labor increases as standards for accuracy, relevance, and importance shift from writer to reader. "Tsk, tsk," readers of our finished work could admonish, "this is not what I wanted."

We don't have similar judgments for first drafts because we have only ourselves to please. First drafts embody who we are, our essence. Sometimes we generate a thousand new ideas. At the birth of each, it is not important which idea will take root and grow to completion. Start many projects and trust that some will flourish.

Several years ago I watched a small thistle grow in our garden. Each day she grew by inches. Soon, blossoms the color of sunrise emerged. Then before I noticed, wind had distributed her seeds. Each seed held her essence. Next season some seeds will sprout and grow in environments that are conducive to a thistle's needs. Other seeds will land and attempt to grow where the environment is unsuitable or where they are not wanted.

"Tsk, tsk, Mr. Seedling," next year's gardener might say. "Grow in the field where you belong, not in my flowerbed."

When we begin projects, our objective is to generalize what we want to create. Often, like the thistle, we don't know the destination of our work. Therefore, our beginner's mind sees what is possible rather than potential mistakes, like the thistle seed that lands in the wrong location. And our beginner's mind does not anticipate possible errors or what is absent from our work.

A friend visited Notre Dame Cathedral in Paris during its reconstruction. He described grandeur. We see what we expect to see, says David Eagleman (2015). My friend glowed with his impressions of the cathedral's architecture, not the scaffolding and workmen. He held a beginner's mind as he visited something he had not witnessed before.

When I sing new songs and play music I have composed for piano, especially at recitals, I perform mostly for myself.

My audience absorbs what they want to hear. They don't experience my mistakes (there are many). Their beginners' minds transcend my "shitty first draft." They enjoy what they expect rather than what actually occurred.

Could you appreciate passion and creative freedom when you begin projects? What would it take to find comfort in the slow growth of your completions? Like the thistle, send a thousand examples of your essence outward on the wind. Some of your ideas will root and grow. Those that do will mature to completion in their own time and in environments that will support you.

Taste What Sustains You

North American black bears sleep through winter in a deep restful state known as torpor. In summer, a female weighs 120 to 180 pounds. To prepare for winter she forages for high fat foods. Nuts, berries, carrion, insects, and small mammals are consumed. She will increase her body weight. Bulky body weight protects mother bear during her long nap. Then she will shed up to thirty percent over winter. In January, she births two or three cubs. A mother bear legend, shared with me in oral tradition by a First People elder who asked to remain anonymous, describes a treat that mother bear offers her cubs as they begin to nurse:

> Mother bear hoards blueberries in her den prior to winter. As she slumbers, she cradles the precious fruit in her paw. When cubs are born, they will taste the berries she protected and consume mother's milk. She provides berries for her cubs' sustenance and mother's milk for their nourishment. When cubs leave the den and climb into the world, they have tasted what will sustain their lives. The imprint of blueberries will guide them as adult bears when they forage for sustenance beyond the

mother's milk they consumed as cubs. So, the legend is told. (source unknown)

∽

Each morning I wake from my slumber to forage for what will sustain my life. Food, family, friends, work, community service, a spiritual life, health, and shelter nourish me. The fruit I have tasted, like the cubs, sustains me. My blueberries are my passions, such as writing and composing music. Although my life is full with nourishment, I am challenged to connect back to the passion for music that sustains me.

Much like the cubs, as children we tasted our passions. Ask children if they are creative and they will say they are. Ask adults and they will likely tell you they are not. What happened as we moved from childhood to adulthood? Ken Robinson in *Finding Your Element* (2014) points to culture and educational systems that promote conformity. We were taught to put round pegs into round holes to meet the needs of our industrialized economy instead of pursuing our creative goals.

Steven Pressfield in *The War of Art* suggests we have a genetic bias toward the pursuit of a creative life. We may feel guilty, however, if we believe we have neglected family or other commitments when we chase personal aspirations. Both are necessary for our sustenance and society at large.

In my youth my mother sustained me with music. She sang English lullabies at bedtime, *Bobby Shafto* among my favorites, as I fought to stay awake but yielded to dreams. My high school band needed horns. Mother encouraged me, so I played trombone. Classical music on our living room piano, another music option, wasn't right for me, so I tasted rock and roll. "I'll be a musician someday," I promised myself as I danced to the piano beat of Jerry Lee Lewis on my portable phonograph in my parent's basement.

About fifty-five years later, at a young seventy years of age, the piano comes full circle when I begin piano lessons. School, marriage, family, home, and career delayed my music ambitions. Over those years, however, I never forgot the taste of my blueberries, the music that sustained me.

In mid-career, I composed lyrics for a rock and roll song. Twenty or so years later in 2014, I co-produced my first music album that included this song and three more. Although the genre of my first song changed from rock and roll, my passion remained firm. The precious fruit passed on to me became songs of my soul cradled, like in mother bear's paw, within my album's protective jacket.

Austin Kleon in *Steal Like an Artist* (2012) describes his experience with a decision to delay a creative passion. He gave up guitar to make time to write a book. Without his guitar, he felt the "phantom limb" he had severed from his creativity. When we seek to be creative, he explains, it is necessary to practice creativity in all aspects of our lives. When we eliminate one or more passions from our lives, we feel loss akin to a missing limb.

When I suspended my music lessons, as I did to write this book, I felt my "phantom limb." This semblance of loss reminded me to return to and taste the fruit that once sustained me. When I write, compose, and perform music, I feel complete. I feel alive. I'm present in creative moments. I will return to music to complete the circle. Thank you, Mother, for the precious fruit that sustains me.

Be Eagle

*W*hen I have too much to accomplish in work and life, I recall my mentor, Cornelia Shipley, when she said, "Richard, who do you need to be to do what you want to do?" To handle more work may not be accomplished with additional knowledge and skills without a change in how we see ourselves with regard to the tasks we face. Cornelia's question challenged me to understand how being supports additional doing.

When in business, I spent most of my career in management. I followed standards and procedures in my work. I achieved success because management requires doing projects right. When we execute projects correctly, we follow prescribed paths. We're tactical and efficient. When goals are clear, we're rewarded with success.

Leadership, on the other hand, means doing projects right and accomplishing the right results. When we finish projects correctly but misjudge outcomes, we lose opportunities to achieve a higher purpose from our work. As we advance in our careers and life, we face more work with broader goals, some unclear. It's not enough to simply do more. In these circumstances, strategy is necessary to achieve a higher purpose than simply task completion.

To be strategic is to lead effectively. Marshall Goldsmith, in *What Got You Here Won't Get You There*, (2007) describes career advancement that begins from the status of a "star performer" who focuses on tactical issues to become a leader, an individual who follows a strategic path. When we lead effectively, we switch from doing to being.

Leadership is a state of being that inspires and motivates others towards strategic goals. When we become leaders, we are recognized by others as leaders. Our ability to inspire, motivate, and gain recognition by those around us is an important characteristic of a leader's state of being.

Prescribed paths and checklists, for example, are valuable for star performers. They're not appropriate for leaders and may be detrimental to their careers. When we're promoted to leadership, focus on ourselves and tactical management will be left behind. These behaviors are replaced by the characteristics of strategic leadership such as empathy and inclusiveness of others. Successful leaders replace me with us. These leaders balance tactical operations of doing with strategic thinking of being.

What are characteristics of being? In 2015 or 2016, a bald eagle soared above US Highway 441 in North Carolina as I drove into Great Smokey Mountains National Park. Revered across cultures, the eagle symbolizes strength and good fortune. Her image adorns national and state flags worldwide. We admire the eagle for who she is and what she represents—her being. And her being is more than who she is. Her being includes what we think about her. What may we learn from eagle?

The eagle soars high above earth. She's among the highest of flyers. In some cultures, the eagle is thought to touch external spiritual places. But she descends to earth to accomplish mortal tasks, such as hunting and scavenging for road kill. The eagle selects a mate for life. She nests on the highest tree. Male and female together raise their young. The stronger of her two chicks may push a weaker sibling from the nest. The eagle's eyesight is eight times stronger than ours. She sees prey from great distances and dives to her target. Unlike other birds of prey, eagle looks forward and backward as she descends. She knows from where she comes and where she goes. Hawk and other raptors, in comparison, never remove their eyes from their target. They focus without discernment.

The eagle balances characteristics of being with doing (strategy with tactics). However, her presence of being is what inspires us. It's no surprise the founders of the United States of America selected the eagle to symbolize who America wanted to be. Our founders could have picked a beaver or turkey, who represent characteristics of doing. Instead, they selected eagle.

How may the eagle support the importance of being for you? Take a problem or issue before you. If you were an eagle, here are six possible characteristic versions of yourself you'd likely need to be:

Visionary. Lead with your values to symbolize who you are. Use your broad wings to elevate you in your career or life to carry you to new places. See what others may not comprehend. Communicate this vision to give meaning to what you do. Lift your mindset beyond day-to-day distractions. If necessary, come down to the weeds. Then soar above obstacles toward your vision.

Loyal. Treat your team as if you're bonded for life. Work together. Credit your group for project success. Personally accept responsibility for failures. Create team purpose. Be a team player, not a star performer.

Focused. Identify what's important and dive for this goal. When we focus from a lofty place, we stay out of the weeds. When we see beyond the mundane, we move toward lofty goals. When we communicate our vision, we engage those around us. With engagement we achieve strategic mission.

Balanced. Learn to efficiently accomplish tactical operations and adjust your actions to effectively achieve higher purpose. Stay in the hunt for an identified target and scavenge for ideas others may have left behind. Be a helper as you clean up after others. Seek centeredness in all phases of your work and life.

Inspirational. Capitalize on your strengths. Lead by example. Be mindful of your shortcomings while you improve who you are. Create opportunities to demonstrate visionary plans and to showcase team competencies. Be purposeful in your pursuit and others will be inspired to follow.

Decisive. Align work and life toward goals. Be firm in your convictions with openness to change. Have flexibility and adjust mid-course plans based on awareness. Keep your eye on goals and look forward and backward to test your convictions.

∽

What would it take for you to be strategic like an eagle? Are you ready to move beyond tactics and elevate your vision and focus on a broader purpose? Who do you need to be to do what you want to do?

Where You Belong

*M*y life is overrun with woodchucks. Right now, one eats seeds below a bird feeder outside the screened-in porch where I write.

"Oh, I see you've discovered our friend." My writing retreat host smiles as she brings birdseed. "She's the big one. There are babies around as well."

I flash back to earlier this year when I discovered holes along the perimeter of the shed behind our residence. Could they be woodchuck burrows? Inspection of the shed revealed a hole gnawed through the wood floor. If he could chew wood, could lawnmower cables and tires be next?

I placed rocks in one entrance to his burrow. He dug another. Then I added rocks and topsoil to the new one so he created a third. What if a skunk or a badger dug the holes and not a woodchuck? To remove a badger would be dangerous. Removal of a skunk would be, ah—tricky. I needed to confirm his identity to decide what to do. Later that week he appeared in my binoculars. Sitting upright in front of the shed, a woodchuck stared at me and squealed.

A woodchuck is a rodent, also known as a groundhog or whistle pig due to the sound they emit when surprised.

A member of a family of large ground squirrels called marmots, woodchucks live at the edge of woodlands. They may invade farms and homes to burrow under buildings and gnaw surroundings with razor sharp, constantly growing incisors. Woodchucks are territorial, difficult to relocate, and will aggressively defend their homes from intruders. What should I do?

"I prefer lead poison," Pete proffered. "I tried a live trap to catch woodchucks in my unfinished basement, but they were wary. I heard they like cantaloupe, but I never tried that. I ended up shooting them."

"Hmm, I don't want to harm the interloper," I mused.

"Leave him alone," Wayne suggested. "Share the shed with him."

I didn't want to cohabitate with a destructive rodent, so I set a live trap baited with cantaloupe. Later that day I escorted him, unharmed, to a field up the road where he belonged.

Years later, I stand in an airplane aisle adjacent to my assigned seat.

"Please be seated, the flight attendant admonishes. "We can't move away from the gate until all passengers are in their assigned locations."

"Is this your book on my seat," I say to the passenger in the adjacent window location, 21E. "I have the aisle in 21D."

"No," says passenger in 21E. "The book belongs to the man who went to the restroom."

"Great," I exclaim. "Overbooked. How will I get home!"

"Excuse me." Man from the restroom squeezes past me, lifts the book from 21D, and sits to face me.

"Excuse me," I say. "Please check your boarding pass. I have 21D reserved."

"No," the man says. "This is my seat and I'm not leaving!"

"Please check your assignment just to be sure," I say.

"Here, check for yourself." He shoves his boarding pass toward me.

"You're in 22D," I say. "This is 21D."

"Oh, my next flight must be 21D," he grumps.

"May I escort you to where you belong?" the flight attendant asks the man.

We'll See

I.

*P*eaceful anti-Vietnam War demonstrations began on college campuses in 1964. Rhetoric and violence peaked in 1970 when Ohio National Guard soldiers shot unarmed Kent State University students. Four were killed and nine wounded.

A Chinese proverb begins with a farmer's horse who breaks from her stable. She escapes to run with a herd of wild horses. When neighbors hear the news, they visit the farmer.

"Oh, what an unfortunate occurrence," one says.

"We'll see." The farmer smiles.

A woodchuck births five pups at my home. They scamper around the lawn and retreat to their burrow as I approach. Like with my earlier woodchuck experience, I bait a live trap with cantaloupe. To expedite removal, I retrieve two more traps from the garage. On my return, one pup has taken the bait.

Enclosed in a wire cage, he screams. Recall that woodchucks are also known as whistle pigs. Nearby, momma woodchuck stands upright. She nibbles grass seemingly oblivious to her pup's dismay. I drive the youngster in his cage to release him in a field of wildflowers on the edge of a stream.

II.

By 1967, Vietnam War demonstrations reach the University of Wisconsin-Milwaukee. One rally begins by chance. I stand with a group of students, street-side, outside the student union. We watch Reserve Officer Training Corps (ROTC) cadets march by.

"USA, USA," they shout.

Like a flock of starlings turning en masse without leadership from any particular bird, the other students and I move from sidewalk to street and march abreast of the ROTC cadets.

"Hell no, we won't go," I chant.

A week after the farmer's mare disappeared, she returns along with three wild stallions. The farmer corrals the herd; neighbors visit.

"Oh, what a fortunate turn of events," a neighbor says.

"We'll see." The farmer smiles.

The morning after I released the woodchuck pup, I trap two more. Momma stands on her haunches and stares into the distance. Again, she seems unconcerned by her youngsters' entrapment and scoots away when I approach. I drive her pups to the same field on the stream.

III.

Cadets and students march side by side until we round a corner. There the street narrows and both groups merge. Surrounded by cadets, like prairie grass that bends with the wind, I stuff hands in my pockets and lower my head.

"USA, USA," I shout.

A week after the farmer's herd grew to four horses, his son tries to break one of the stallions. He falls from his mount and fractures a leg. When neighbors learn of the accident, they visit.

"Oh, what an unfortunate mishap," one says.

"We'll see." The farmer smiles.

On the third morning of woodchuck removal, I trap the last two pups. Momma still stands tall. Her gaze fixates beyond the horizon. What does she see? What does she sense? I release the pups in the same location.

IV.

As cadets and students continue their march, the street eventually widens. Both groups separate. Back among the students, like a pigeon returning home, I raise my head, hands, and fists.

"Hell no, we won't go," I yell.

One week after the farmer's son broke his leg, soldiers enter the village.

"All young men line up here," the captain shouts. "You will fight in the Emperor's war."

The farmer wheels his injured son in a cart to the front of the line.

"He is not needed," the captain says.

After soldiers leave the village, neighbors congregate.

"Oh, what a favorable event," a neighbor says.

"We'll see." The farmer smiles.

Momma woodchuck takes the bait, cantaloupe there delivers her fate. She rides to a stream, to realize her dream. In wildflowers, her children await.

Be Yourself

A client I mentor, whom I'll call Gabe, seeks passion in his work but doesn't have words to express what he wants. A part-time musician and full-time accountant, Gabe feels stuck in his career.

"I'm just an accountant," he laments. "I don't see anything special in my work."

"Be yourself," I say. "Passion, and the life you want, will find you."

"How will passion find me?"

"Gabe, can you remember a time in your life when you were excited about your work? Maybe you felt in the flow? When this happened, did hours pass like minutes? When you finished what you set out to do, did you want to repeat the activity? Can you name your passion in that moment?"

"That's difficult," he says. "I want to discover my passions, but I don't know where to begin."

"When we don't know where to begin, we start with what we know," I say. "Gabe, may I share a story that might help you define your career?"

He nods and settles back in his chair.

"I've searched to define my musical genre. Like you feel

you are just an accountant and want more, I knew I was more than just a one-genre musician. The music industry, especially producers, publishers, and record labels in their day, like to put musicians in a box for business reasons. Oh, he plays rock and roll, or she sings country, for example. The industry is uncomfortable with genre crossovers and hybrid musicians. These artists are seen as more work and greater risk for producers. The message to musicians is to sing yesterday's song rather than experiment with tomorrow's music."

"Yes, a business model rather than an artist's approach," Gabe chimes. "My profession is similar and much of what we do is government regulated. Innovation is inadvertently discouraged. Maybe that's life, too. Nature doesn't like differences. She emulates sameness. Please continue, Richard."

"Astute remarks, Gabe. Thank you. Yes, uniformity. Although nature requires uniformity for species to live in the short term, mutations are necessary for long term survival. For me, as a new musician, I wanted to find my long term genre. Was my music the same or different from the rest? As a writer for most of my life, I gravitated to song lyrics in the 1970s. Usually written in journals, my early songs were composed without music, similar to poems. Around 2011 and through 2013, I picked my best lyrics and collaborated with Conni Blomberg on piano and lyrics, Mike Vial on guitar and music (melody and bassline) and other singers and musicians to create my first album, *Going Home*, produced in 2014. You know what?"

"Say more," Gabe replies.

"The album included four songs in as many genres. None of the songs represented the type of music I wanted to write, compose, and produce for the next part of my music career.

I wanted future albums to include songs written, composed, performed, and produced by me, not songs composed and performed by others as I did in *Going Home*. I wanted to be a singer-songwriter similar to those in the 1970s. However, I didn't know how to classify my new music, so I asked my music instructor to name my genre. Nancy told me, 'Your music is you. There's no genre for what you do.'"

"Oops." Gabe laughs. "Dead end, but maybe a start for something different?"

"Right, Gabe. For fun I checked music genres on iTunes. They listed standard music genres, such as folk, rock, country, jazz, blues, soul, and an endless list of names that musicians use to define their work. An iTunes list is other people's work, not mine."

"So, if I extrapolate your message so far..." Gabe says. "What I want to do in my career, my music, so to speak, may not fit a standard definition. But my work and my passion should be what I want to do in the future, not what someone else thinks I should do."

"Exactly!" I high five Gabe. "Just because what you want to do doesn't have a name, that doesn't prevent you from naming the parts of what you do. For example, when I'm in the flow, I compose my best work. I'm passionate. When I'm passionate, I'm bold. I take risks. At one particular creative moment, for fun I identified one of my musical genres as Engelbert Humperdinck meets Deep House."

"Ha!" Gabe exclaims. "You are a crooner in an electronic dance music format, quite an unlikely combination. How did you come up with that?"

"Simple. I began with the vocal part of my music. Engelbert is a lounge style singer from the late 1960s, as you know. His music, vocal range, and love songs remind me of his contemporary, Tom Jones. Both men sing elongated, mellow-toned vowels. When I sing at my best, my voice emulates them. Here's the other part of my discovery. Deep House is today's version of House music. I loved House music in the 1970s and 1980s. Deep House is also known as Chill music. Chill includes extended chords (7ths, 9ths, and 11ths) instead of standard triad chords. Deep House melodies have an ambient, unrelated feel similar to jazz that suggests to listeners to *chill out.*"

"Okay, for me, it's not enough to say I'm just an accountant then," Gabe says. "Like with your music, I'm more than that. So, if I name what I do best in my career, the parts of my work that give me passion, as you describe it, such as being like a smoke jumper putting out my client's fires, then I'll know what parts of my career are destined for me."

"Yes, you're a smoke jumper. You solve your client's problems. That's one part of you that comes from your passion. For me, once I gained confidence to name the parts of what I passionately created and boldly combined them into a new description, no matter how crazy it sounded, my music no longer felt like a mishmash of unrelated chords and notes. With names for the parts of my music, I realized that I had a unique identity for the whole of what I created."

"I get it," Gabe exclaims. "Name the parts of what I love in my career when I perform at my best. Similar to iTunes, I don't need standard definitions to determine who I am. If I name parts of my career that come from my passions, then my future is unlimited. The job, career, and life that's right for me, just like your music, will find me if I just be me."

Life Is Like Music

"Life is like music," William says.

I coach him, a healthcare clinic manager, on staffing issues. When William isn't at the clinic, evenings usually find him behind his keyboard with his band at local music venues.

"Tell me more, William," I respond.

"Here's what I mean. All notes need to be heard. For example, I often compose piano music in the key of C major. If my melody includes an F major chord and I want to finish my song, I usually take my music directly to a C major chord. This transition is the quickest way to finish my tune because I hear two compatible major chords that suggest completion.

"Other times," he continues, "I move my melody from F major through E minor and D minor to C major. This progression is less direct than my usual choice. The additional minor chords also build tension in the melody. Unlike major chords that bring completion to music, minor chords keep a listener in suspension because minor chords sound incomplete or suggest a slowdown in the music."

"Hmm, I feel a problem in the works," I muse.

"Yes." William chuckles. "We want to improve customer service at the clinic. When a patient calls for a prescription refill, for example, nursing assistants write the refill order. Pretty routine. Nursing assistants are authorized to renew medicine. However, if other non-emergency health issues are identified, nursing assistants must refer patients to a registered nurse or doctor. A nurse or doc will then return the patient's call later that day or early the next."

"Okay, your policy seems reasonable. What's the issue?"

"Here's the problem, Management wants nursing assistants to follow the protocol I described. However, assistants have different ideas on how to improve customer service. Let's go back to my example. A patient calls to renew a prescription. A nursing assistant discovers a possible need for other, non-emergency care. Nursing assistants want more immediate follow up by a nurse or doctor on the secondary patient issue. Think of nursing assistants as minor chords and nurses or doctors as major chords in our healthcare system.

"When nursing assistants request more timely return of calls," William continues, "like the minor chords on my piano, they create tension in our company. Immediate return of calls might require additional work or create schedule problems for doctors or nurses. I feel that an effective solution to this issue, one that acknowledges the views of the assistants, could improve customer service. Maybe there's a compromise such as return of calls within two hours."

"You're caught in the middle," I say.

"Yes. Assistants have first contact with customers, and they are key to effective patient management. We call them *customer facing*. We need nursing assistant ideas, and I want their input."

"So," I say. "What blocks a stronger voice for customer-facing individuals in your organization?"

"Look at it this way. My boss and I represent clinic leadership. Organizationally, we report to headquarters. The company wants quick, low-cost solutions. To return to my piano analogy, we are major chords along with doctors and nurses in our business. Headquarters wants us to go directly, so to speak, from F major to C major with our current patient protocol. However, when we apply a quick conclusion to a phone call and make a referral, like the major chord progression in my analogy, we are efficient in short-term patient management but ineffective in long-term customer care.

"Because nursing assistants are minor chords in my analogy," William continues, "assistants' voices enrich our service delivery music. But in a centralized leadership structure, such as ours, strong voices of the majority (the major chords) are dominant. I want to incorporate the voices of the minority (the minor chords). Unless we listen to assistants' recommendations, we'll miss long-term critical patient needs and fail to achieve the vision of excellence within our organization."

"William, I'm pleased to hear you deliver an eloquent argument to incorporate minority voices in your clinic operations. You need the tension of the minor chords. They balance the dominance and bias toward resolution of the major chords. Minor chords help you reach alternative solutions that accommodate different viewpoints. Maybe the compromise you describe is possible because minor chords are in your music? Your customers want all voices to be heard."

One-Act Play

A moment of presence is a one-act play. In the business world, one of the top attributes of a brand is customer experience. Consistency of experience creates brand loyalty. A loyal customer is a repeat customer. Typically, repeat business is a lower cost opportunity for higher profit margins than new business. Customer retention, therefore, should be a preferred business priority. But people and business operations are imperfect. Mistakes happen. When a loyal customer is disappointed in *Scene One*, how a business could have responded in *Scene Two* is an opportunity to strengthen the company's brand.

Scene One

"I'd like a twelve-ounce, dark roast coffee and oatmeal with raisins, almonds, honey, and skim milk, please," I say.

"I'm sorry." The barista shakes his head. "We don't have oatmeal this morning. We have to go to 7-Eleven to get oatmeal."

"Okay, I guess I'll come back another time." I shrug. How annoying. I look at him in silence. I want oatmeal. Why didn't you buy oatmeal yesterday? Or you could have picked it up this morning before I arrived. The 7-Eleven store is right across the street. Why weren't you prepared?

"Would you still like your coffee," he says

"No thanks," I say

He stares at me in silence.

I leave.

Comment

What's wrong in Scene One from a customer experience point of view? The barista's script was an excuse, not an apology. Besides saying "I'm sorry," an apology should include a recognition of how the mistake has affected the customer. Also, some type of amends or assurance should be offered to show how the error will be avoided in the future.

The barista's script also described business issues, not customer concerns. Explanations of why oatmeal wasn't available is of little interest to the customer, and the barista's reasons reinforced the already negative experience. The business lost a sale and possibly a customer. Let's replay this interaction in Scene Two with a positive experience script.

Scene Two

"I'd like a twelve-ounce, dark roast coffee and oatmeal with raisins, almonds, honey, and skim milk, please," I say.

"I'm sorry." The barista shakes his head. "We don't have oatmeal this morning. We have fresh baked scones, cookies, and other breakfast items. Would you like a free cup of coffee to go with your selection?"

"Wow, how thoughtful. I'd love a scone, and thanks for free coffee."

"It's the least we can do. I'm grateful you're a regular customer. I've made a note to check oatmeal supply once a week. See you tomorrow."

"Yes, you will." I sit and enjoy my breakfast.

What Is?

*W*hen lonely on a Saturday evening in the late 1960s, I would telephone home on Sunday night. Long distance rates were cheaper on Sunday. What's the cost of love? How to decide?

Think of a bell curve for information to make a decision. As a young boy and teenager, I needed little to make a choice (the start of the bell curve). Remember *Mad Magazine*'s mascot, Alfred E. Neuman? His gap-toothed grin graced nearly all of the American humor magazine's 550 covers that began in 1956 with his slogan, "What, me worry?" Same for me.

In my twenties and thirties, I ramped up worry (the middle of the bell curve). I sought increasingly more information to make decisions. My thirst for facts, or what I assumed to be truth, probably peaked in my forties. Today, in the later part of my life (the far side of the bell curve), I need less information from others. I'm comfortable with ambiguity. I realize "we control nothing, but influence everything," as Brian Klaas eloquently states in Fluke: *Chance, Chaos, and Why Everything We Do Matters* (2024). My truth now comes from inside of me. Let's go back to my life in the 1950s to see how this change came to be.

I grew up passive, afraid to take a stand, striving to blend in and not attract attention by being vague in word and deed. With answers to Dad's questions that were not quite right, for example, I could be okay with him but, more importantly, never wrong. How shameful to make an error!

When I faced a choice, often another person's opinion would suffice. Or a bit more information would be enough. "Just the facts, ma'am," as Sgt. Joe Friday frequently said on the *Dragnet* TV series. I relied on opinions of others that I assumed to be facts or their confirmation of my ideas to help me make decisions.

"Right, Dad," I usually said at the end of most of our dinner table conversations. His confirmation of my thoughts worked for years until he caught on to my gambit.

"Why do you always seek my approval?" He frowned. "Don't you have ideas of your own?"

Indeed, I did. I wrote my thoughts in passive voice, still striving not to be wrong. I received *A* grades in college classes where finals were essay exams. I advanced childhood skills to dodge requested accuracy. I penned answers to exam questions based on what I wanted to write about, rather than what the instructor asked. When I linked my answers with a thread to the actual question posed, my essays were not quite right to the query, but never wrong. The art of the essay.

Popular culture during my childhood also groomed me to seek confirmation. At an early age I learned that boys should understand the world or at least know what is in front of us. Recall Mrs. Chapman, my Cub Scout den mother. She recited the Cub Scouts' motto, "Be prepared." Prepared for what? Even when I didn't know as a Cub Scout, and later as a teenager, or was not quite sure, I was given examples of how to pretend to know. Dad knew where he was driving (or he thought he did) even when he was lost. Eventually, I learned that information, as well as third-party confirmations and opinions in passive voice, were necessary to make better decisions.

In the 1970s I stayed home on Saturday nights with the Sunday edition of the *Chicago Tribune* instead of dinner, a night on the town, or perhaps a date with someone special.

"Richard, you could read the *Trib* on Saturday nights, so you don't have to be alone."

The office secretary, whom I'll call Linda, had a smile as warm as the mug of coffee I held. "I'll finish typing your report for your review later today." She locked her eyes on mine, ran long, slender fingers through her jet-black hair, and turned back to her typewriter.

Available after five o'clock in the evening on Saturday, the Saturday night edition of the *Chicago Tribune* included financial pages, sports, *Parade Magazine*, Mike Royko's column (the crusading columnist), and everything I'd read on Sunday except for late breaking news. A special edition that hit the street after eleven o'clock on Saturday evenings included current news. I read the Saturday night early edition for maximum information twelve hours before everyone else. I prepared myself. Thank you, Mrs. Chapman.

Before I spent Saturday nights with Mike Royko, I devoured magazines and evening television news in my broader search for more information. Many in my generation believed in the truth presented by Walter Cronkite, the charismatic CBS evening news anchor with his signature sign-off. "And that's the way it is."

Why wouldn't I believe in Walter's message? I never

asked if it was really that way. And what was it? Did he imply acceptance of what I witnessed because I had no choice? For me to ignore what seemed obvious from what he stated as factual would suggest I denied reality. I accepted, therefore, what he said as reality. But what is reality?

Is my dream life less real than my life while awake? Is perception of my waking life less real than yours? Recall the potential conflict between what we want to see and what we actually observe—I'll return to this topic later regarding factual and emotional truth.

Or did Walter present a challenge for his audience with the implication, "If you don't like *what is*, do something about it"? I wasn't ready to proactively challenge authority, so I accepted what he stated. Even when he reported Pentagon-produced Vietcong body counts that seemed unrealistic, I trusted the accuracy of his information.

I saw the sun rise every morning, for example, and set in the evening. I noticed the sun performed her daily duty just as I witnessed Walter's performance. I believed in both. The sun didn't lie, so why would Walter Cronkite report false information?

My willingness to accept what I was told as truth was also used by authority figures who tried to explain reality. Mr. Johnson, at Nicolet, uttered meaningless phrases such as, "Boys will be boys." His words implied that inexplicable behavior could be justified as predictable or natural, like my observation of the sun. Boys will be boys because boys can't change. Remember the phrase, "Pictures don't lie?" We now know photographs may be manipulated, and some people create deep fakes. We also understand that boys may change, myself included.

When we could still trust photographs, we also trusted what we read. As a preteen, I remember dinner table conversation about which newspapers reported the truth. We assumed only one truth. Years later I believed in the accuracy of the *Chicago Tribune,* and Dad would have trusted *The New York Times,* if he had read *The Times.* This is not to say that both were trustworthy; rather, the culture of the time was to believe in mass media accuracy. We trusted the third estate because we had not yet defined truth as dependent on political bias or situational to an individual. I tended to believe what I read even when mundane.

One day in the 1980s, I sipped vending machine coffee from a Styrofoam cup in Milwaukee's Amtrak terminal. Scratched plexiglass windows failed to block the late summer's oppressive heat. Clatter from railroad yard operations beyond metal-paneled terminal walls echoed from concrete floors that stretched to the terminal's arrival and departure gates. I fingered a soft cellophane-wrapped donut while Dad and I waited on straight-backed wood benches for my train to Chicago on Milwaukee Road's Hiawatha Line.

"Why did they build the freeway on the old depot's site?" I turned to Dad. "This terminal isn't as nice as the old station on Lake Michigan."

"Money, I guess, or community opposition," Dad said "Maybe people in the high-rise condominiums along the lake didn't want to look at the old railroad station."

"Thanks for the donut." I sighed. "I'll save it for later."

"Wait here, Richard. I'll get you a sandwich from the vending machine. You'll be hungry on the train or when you get home." He returned with a ham sandwich, December, stamped on the cellophane wrapper.

"This sandwich is either very old or quite fresh." I laughed. "I'm hungry; I'll guess fresh."

Like with the December sandwich, we observe what we want to see. I saw in Walter Cronkite a father-like presence that strengthened his believability. His persuasive manner created an aura of unvarnished truth. And his words were captured by my ears, eager to believe in the contemporary wisdom exemplified in the name of a popular TV sit-com in the 1960s, *Father Knows Best.* I never questioned if my father truly knew what was best.

Today, I have come full circle. I believe in acceptance but only to the point where I see few suitable alternatives. "That's the way it is," has become my call to action. Walter Cronkite challenged me, many years ago, to ask why and to think for myself. I didn't understand his guidance at the time, however, nor did I have sufficient self-confidence to accept my own truth until now.

Today, I understand the difference between factual and personal truth. Personal truth resides within me and not from the factual data I've been given. And, as with the December sandwich, what are the facts? Political discourse refers to "alternative facts." We've seen how facts may be manipulated for election purposes. And Joe Friday's "facts" are no longer mine. Nor are Walter Cronkite's Pentagon-produced Vietcong body count facts mine. I continue my work to eliminate the residue of the adolescent lie I've carried, my belief about not being enough, the most inhibiting fact that I've carried. Instead of the lie I've believed, I look for my personal truth (my reality and my definition of what is). My personal truth is my emotional truth.

Wendy Fontaine is the author of "Why You Should Write

About What You Don't Remember" (Pagliarulo and Talarico, 2021), an inspiring essay on factual and emotional truth. She describes the process of writing her memoir. She *remembers* the ordeal of her divorce and the loss of her family as a winter event. Years later, she discovers that her divorce happened in mid-summer. Rather that re-writing her memoir and "being slavish to the facts," as Ms. Fontaine describes, she stays with her memory of a winter divorce, her emotional truth. For the author, winter is the season of loss, cold, and colorless days. How relevant is the fact of a summer divorce compared to the emotional truth of a winter divorce for her? Both are true, but what's more important?

Think of factual truth as left brain (doing) and emotional truth as right brain (being). Recall how we see the flow of the Wisconsin River today based on what we want to observe or what we believe. We hold that vision until we change our perspective. With a change in point of view, like when the geologists witnessed evidence from aerial photographs that the river flowed in the opposite direction in the distant past, our eyes are opened to possibility, and we see, maybe for the first time, new clues allowing us to discard old beliefs. Memories often take the form of beliefs. Memories, like beliefs, may be changed.

Maybe Coach Wagner didn't discover that I needed glasses to see the baseball (factual truth)? I liked Mr. Wagner, a kind and encouraging father-type of man. My mentor. Perhaps I wanted him to help me (emotional truth) more than he actually did. Maybe Mrs. Higgins advised my mother that I needed glasses instead of Mr. Wagner. I remember my first-grade teacher as harsh and critical, not helpful. What if both happened? What if neither happened? I wear glasses to this day. Since no one was hurt and I feel better about my memory of Mr. Wagner being there for me instead of Mrs. Higgins, does this factual truth matter? One more example.

Recall my earlier essay, "What's True," in which I experienced three alternative realities near the old barn. After I described my first encounter, my mother sent me to my room to "remember what really happened." I wanted to please her, so I remembered events differently. To this day I remember fear, my emotional truth. Circumstances of the events (facts) don't really matter.

In Gabor Maté's groundbreaking research and reporting on Western Medicine's scientific methods (typically defined as facts) in *The Myth of Normal* (2022), he describes trauma as our body's response to external events. Unlike conventional definitions of trauma as centered on what happened, Dr. Maté maintains that facts don't matter. What's important is how we change in response to precipitating events. He further argues in a video series titled *The Wisdom of Trauma*, that the body copes with traumatic occurrences through memory blocks and imagined situations. We imagine what the body needs to heal.

Similar to Gabor Maté, Vivian Gornick, in *Situation and Story* (2021), separates a causal event that she defines as the "situation" from the story. We all may experience the same or a similar event, but each person will put a personal spin on the situation that will become their story. There will be as many stories as there are individuals and typically fewer situations.

Memory is not a score-keeping function of a healthy body. Memory, rather, serves the body based on what the body needs. Some memories, therefore, may need to be changed.

Emotional truth is accurate to the body. But emotional truth could be misleading about what the body requires. That's why examination and reflection through presence are important. Similar examination of factual truth is also necessary. My answer to "*what is*" comes from this process of reflection, of being present.

On reflection, should I have called home when lonely on Saturday nights even though phone rates were cheaper on Sunday?

"We'll see." The farmer smiles.

Father and Son

I'm his son, the only one.
He's the one, his father's son.
Earth and sun, never undone.
Single one, father and son.

*W*ho am I other than the son of countless fathers before me? Who do I blame for what never worked out in my life? Should I congratulate myself for a life well lived? May I have this conundrum both ways? I choose not. I'm responsible for my life.

Kate Meadows is author of "The Quiet Memoir: Finding Conflict in a "Quiet" Life" (Pagliarulo and Talarico, 2021), an inciteful essay on her struggles to find meaning through conflict in her writing. She describes her uneventful life in Wyoming absent abuse, addiction, and violence that she assumes are necessary ingredients for a successful memoir. Instead, she writes of her quiet life without extreme trauma, probably more similar for most of us than a life of physical and emotional duress.

My life is a quiet one. No major family events dogged me. Yes, ordinary setbacks mattered. And, I've been shaped by many people, Dad included.

Wesley Frank Wilberg was my dad, a good father and family provider. Although his words of affection were rare, I felt love through his actions. I've described him as a "cool dude," neither all bad nor all good. Just a man who happened to be my father. Popular descriptions of father-son relationships such as "the apple doesn't fall far from the tree" don't apply. To understand who I am, over the years I've compared myself to him.

We are similar in some respects. I default to blaming others, for example. I'm working on that. And I have his optimistic outlook. We differ, however, more than we are similar. Politics is our major difference. Further comparisons have limited value. What's more important is who shaped Dad.

Dad's father was Frank Wilberg, born in Friedland, Mecklenburg, Germany, in 1888. Frank married Meta Boesche in 1912 in New York. Dad, born three years later, was their only child. Meta died in Milwaukee in 1935 when Dad was twenty years old. Meta shaped Dad through her life and death. Dad spoke of her often. In my youth we visited her grave on most Mother's Days. Recall when Meta influenced me later in my life.

Frank next married Orra Garschke in March 1946, one month after her husband, John died. But Frank had known Orra at least twelve years prior to their marriage. Orra described meeting Frank at a dance (she didn't say when) in an article published in the *Hi-Desert Star* of Yucca Valley, California, in September 1980. She said, "Mr. Wilberg had a teenage son, and he asked her to marry him." Dad's teenage years were from 1928 to 1934, while Frank was married to Meta and before Meta's death.

Dad never bonded with Orra. He described her as "a

married woman." Yes, Orra was married to John Garshke, but he had been committed to the Milwaukee County Asylum for the Chronic Insane from at least 1930. Orra and her children likely lived with Frank during part of John's confinement.

The U.S. Census for 1940 lists Frank's residence at 803 East Wells Street in Milwaukee. He's cited as married to "Meta" even though Meta died five years earlier. Frank is noted as the apartment building manager at his residence. There are no records of residency for Orra Garschke or Orra Wilberg, but Ora's adult son, Robert Garry, lived next door to Frank at 813 East Wells Street.

Orra shaped Dad through her secret life with Frank; some of that time could have been before Dad left home to marry my mother in 1938. Maybe his coolness toward Orra is more about normal adjustments in a blended family than anything Orra did. Or maybe Dad misplaced his anger with Frank toward Orra about use of Meta's name for Orra.

I have childhood memories of Frank's country home when he lived with Orra in Mukwonago, Wisconsin, in the late 1940s and early 1950s. On one occasion Dad gave Frank an outboard motor for his fishing boat. Frank later sold the motor and didn't tell Dad. Dad became angry when he heard about the sale. Years later I gave an outboard motor to Dad. Dad subsequently gifted the motor to Doug and didn't inform me. Later, when I learned about the gift, I too became angry. Maybe the apple…?

Additional memories of Frank are from my early adolescence when Frank and Orra operated a motel named Le-Orra Court in Joshua Tree, California. In addition to innkeeper duties, Frank prospected for gold in adjacent foothills. He found a pinch or two of gold dust that he kept in a small glass vial. To my untrained eyes, the sample resembled sand. We searched his many claims and found considerably more sand, but nothing that Frank called gold.

Dad's relationship with Frank was more like sand than gold. The outboard motor incident suggested a deeper conflict. Dad never talked about why they didn't get along except for Orra being married. Did Dad blame Frank for Frank's relationship with Orra and see it as an affront to Meta, although she was deceased? When Dad spoke of Frank, usually he described his father's many occupations and locations where the family lived instead of anything deeper. Was Dad's friction with Frank due to important differences? Their politics were opposite, but both were Lutheran and Masons. Frank achieved a Masonic Rosicrucian degree (belief in alchemy among other practices) but Dad was never an active Mason. Where Dad declared himself an atheist later in life, Frank pursued other spiritual practices that later in his life included membership in the Mentalphysics Institute in Joshua Tree.

Most important of what I know about Frank's relationship with Dad, however, and how he may have shaped Dad is hinted in Frank's Last Will and Testament. He wrote that there shall be no sadness, weeping, or display of emotions at his memorial service. Frank died in 1970 at Hi-Valley Memorial Hospital in Yucca Valley. Memorial services were held at the Mentalphysics Retreat Center in Joshua Tree. His remains were likely buried at Joshua Tree Memorial Park even though Frank owned an unused burial plot next to Meta at Pinelawn in Milwaukee.

Dad didn't mourn Frank's death, nor did he attend his father's memorial service.

"Too far to drive," he said.

In 1963, before Frank passed on, he mailed me a hand-written history of the Wilberg family. The cover page addressed the document to me. Years later I wondered why Frank named me to receive the family lineage and why he bypassed Dad. More years later, after Dad died and within six months after Mother followed, I administered their joint estate. In their Last Will and Testament, written by Dad and agreed to by Mother, they declared their estate to be divided equally between my sister and me and three grandchildren. A will that names a trust or third parties such as grandchildren is said to bypass a direct descendent. We will see how the Wilberg family history was passed from grandfather to grandson for several generations, in essence fathers bypassed sons. Does this pattern of information dissemination suggest that sons could have been bypassed by fathers in other ways as well, such as regarding emotional support?

If Frank emotionally bypassed Dad in his life, could Frank have been emotionally bypassed by his father, Erdman Wilberg? What I know about Erdman is his birth in Friedland in 1858, prior to the creation of the modern German nation in 1871. He worked as a barber and carpenter and had four children that included Frank. I don't have any evidence of possible family turmoil to influence Frank until I go further back to Erdman's father, Albert Wilberg.

Albert, was also born in Friedland; his birthdate and date of death are unknown. Albert's father, name unknown, was born somewhere in the Germanic states in 1825. Frank handwrote about Albert in the family history (in his words except where I have noted for clarity):

My grandfather, Albert Wilberg was very well educated—that is self-educated, as he never had any schooling. He was one of 12 children and his father died when he was small. He was a herdsman for the geese of the town when he was a boy. (I assume Frank refers to Albert). Borrowed books when he could get them and knew all flowers by its Latin name. When he was over 80 years old, he recited many very lengthy peoms (poems) to me. He was 88 when he died… It has been traced that the name used to be "von Wilberg" and the family had a castle on the Hundsruck which is a part of the Vosges (Vogesen) mountain range in South West Germany. All such names as the following should be included in further research: Wilberg, Wildberg, Willberg, Wilberger, Wilburg, Wilbert and Wilber… The story handed down by my grandfather Albert Wilberg was that his great grandvather (grandfather) was born and raised at the castle as "von Wilberg". He and his brother were in love with the same girl, and our ancestor killed his brother in a dual (duel). His title was taken away and he was bannished (banished) from the castle. He traveled and finally settled in Friedland, Mecklenburg.

Whoa, I said I had a quiet life. I did, and I'll explain my take on the duel later. But first, did Albert's father emotionally bypass Albert? If so, maybe Albert's father was bypassed by his father (the victor in the reported duel), and so on before him. Dr. Richard C. Schwartz in *No Bad Parts* (2021) describes intergenerational family trauma as "legacy burdens." Recall that events don't have to be horrific to invoke trauma, especially for those with a quiet life.

Epigenetic studies of laboratory mice by Kerry Ressler and Brian Dias at Emory University, first reported by Dias in 2013, suggest that family trauma may be inherited and thereby, according to the author, "learned." Researchers exposed male and female mice to cherry blossom fragrance and simultaneously gave the mice an electric shock. Exposed mice were measured for body reactions during the experience and subsequently mated. Offspring (pups) who had never previously experienced cherry blossom fragrance were exposed to this odor. Pups had similar measured-body reactions as their parents. They learned fear of cherry blossoms, a trans-generational trauma (legacy burdens), from their parents.

Resmaa Menakem, in *My Grandmother's Hands: Racialized Trauma and the Pathway to Mending Our Hearts and Bodies* (2017), gives a hopeful message about trauma passed from generation to generation. We have the capacity to break the chain of family trauma when we become aware of how we continue legacy burdens. When we take personal responsibility for our lives, we become change agents and not victims of our traumas. In that way we heal our legacy burdens and change the future for others.

Now back to the duel. Recall the difference between factual truth and emotional truth. Frank remembered stories told to him by Albert. Recall that we hear what we want to hear and we remember what is meaningful. The mind is a meaning-making machine. Frank remembers Albert's stories just as Albert remembers what was told to him. What if Albert's story of the duel wasn't true (factual truth). Albert tells the story to Frank who describes the story to me, so maybe they had faith in the accuracy of their accounts (their emotional truths). Notice that Frank says "traced"—that implies accuracy rather than "alleged" or "rumored" in his writing of the story. If Frank and Albert's emotional truth is belief in the accuracy of the story, then they could have had something to gain from retelling the story. Maybe they received attention or had someone to blame for their lives or felt better about themselves. No one knows.

What I do know about Dad and Frank, however, is that both had many unrelated jobs as opposed to careers. Maybe as a result, and due to experiences of The Great Depression, both were drawn toward get-rich-quick schemes. Frank was also an unsuccessful inventor in addition to being a gold miner, and Dad had a vivid imagination. He often embellished factual truth, especially in fishing stories. What if Dad and Frank learned these characteristics in order to survive, like the mice learned about cherry blossoms? What if Albert imagined, while he watched geese (uneventful when wolves were absent), what his life could have been like if he or his ancestors had lived in a castle? What if Albert believed that he wasn't enough, like the lie I told myself? Legacy burdens haunt us until we change our memories.

I began to change memories of Dad in 2012, when I started to blog stories about him. Over subsequent years, I saw Dad's trauma and his connections to the world as legacy burdens. What if Dad believed he wasn't enough, and I shared his legacy burdens? In my blogs, I replaced blame toward him with compassion. Many of my stories became essays that are included in this book. A writing peer, after she read several blogs, called my stories "love letters to your father." Perhaps. Maybe the following is one more love letter.

I fished with Dad on a hot summer day in 2002 or 2003 before he "walked on." I manned a rowboat that day (no outboard motor). Previously we fished from shore or walked in shallows in rubber boots or chest-high waders. Dad's swollen legs now prevented shoreline fishing. He spent most of his days in the nursing home bed or reclined in a chair by a window, so he eagerly agreed to fish from a boat.

"This is the best fishing day ever," he said near the end of the day.

"Why?" I shook my head. "We didn't catch any fish."

"I got to spend the day with you." He looked at me. "This is probably the last time we'll fish."

He was right.

Chronic Acts of Friendship

*D*ad would talk to anyone, even Kenny Rogers. No kidding, Kenny Rogers. Quite an embarrassment, actually. Not about Kenny Rogers but because of Dad's chronic acts of friendship. He'd walk up to a stranger on the street, for example, and without any reason strike a familiar gambit.

"Hi, I'm Wes Wilberg. What's your name?"

I'd shrink to a body size smaller than my youthful frame could accommodate. Dad's outsized personality was likely due to his variety of occupations, including used car salesman.

"Ain't she a beaut?" he would say. "I see you driving this baby home tonight." As a child of The Great Depression, his survival depended on friendship with everyone. The biggest reason for Dad's pattern of seeking new relationships, however, was his desire to make someone's day a little bit better; that included his own.

I wasn't with him the day he met Kenny Rogers, but here's the story Dad later told me about his conversation on a summer day in the 1990s:

"Hi buddy." Dad greeted a man in the parking garage at the Pfister Hotel in downtown Milwaukee. "Nice van you've got there."

"Hey, yourself. I'm Kenny Rogers. I use the van while my band is on tour."

"Kenny Rogers?" Dad grinned. "Yeah, sure, and I'm Bill Clinton."

"No kidding. I am Kenny Rogers. We perform at Summerfest tonight. Okay, Bill, what's your real name? Here's a couple of tickets to the show if you fess up."

"Wes Wilberg. Thanks Kenny. You've made my day."

"Go ahead, make my day," said Clint Eastwood, who played Harry Callahan, the ruthless San Francisco police department inspector in the 1983 crime thriller *Sudden Impact*, when he pointed a .44 caliber Magnum revolver in the face of a criminal.

Fortunately, it won't take a bad guy to make my day about twenty-five or more years after Kenny Rogers made Dad's day. Instead, on an afternoon when blue sky never ended for me, a small, mangy, black-and-white dog and a stranger, whom I'll call Ron Peterson, will make my day.

The dog scampers out of a cornfield near Barneveld, Wisconsin, and sprints across four lanes of traffic on US Highway 18 directly in front of me. I swerve to avoid the mutt. She bolts up a grassy slope and drops to rest in front of a Kwik Trip convenience mart. I take her lead and pull in for gas.

I stare at the dog as I pump fuel. She backs away from my gaze. A biker dude dressed in durag, denim, chains, and black leather boots pulls in for gas. He parks at the next fuel island between me and doggie and leans his black Harley Davidson V-twin Low Rider on its kickstand. Chrome gleams in the sun.

His bike is complete with saddlebags, ape hanger handlebars, and sissy bar where he's strapped a sleeping bag and probably extra clothing, rain gear, guns, booze, and drugs. He must be headed to Sturgis, South Dakota, for the motorcycle rally to terrorize residents or to raise hell with his outlaw buddies in some other small Midwestern town.

He tosses something to the dog. I want to meet this dude because I also own a Harley. To stroll across thirty feet of asphalt unarmed and unprepared for a possible confrontation might be dangerous. Instead, I drive over to the dude, lower the window, and let my engine idle.

"Hi, buddy. I saw you toss something to the pooch." My hands tighten on the steering wheel.

"She looks hungry but won't eat the rest of my sandwich." He turns from doggie to me. "She seems frightened and lost. I'm concerned about her."

"Yeah, I almost hit her just before I stopped for gas." I watch her retreat over the top of the embankment. "Where you headed?"

"Nebraska."

"Wow, you've got a long ride." I keep my right foot close to the car's gas pedal.

"Yup. Left Appleton this morning. If weather holds, I'll make Hastings, Nebraska, by dark. I've planned a week or two with Mom. I teach high school, so I have summers off. She's eighty-eight now and appreciates my visits. In my saddlebags I have cheese, bratwurst, and other Wisconsin delicacies she loves."

"You're a great son." I step out of the car and offer my hand. "What's your name?"

"Ron Peterson," he says.

"I'm Richard Wilberg. Great to meet you, Ron. Have a safe trip."

I get back into my car and head for the highway. In my rearview mirror, doggie nibbles Ron's sandwich. He rubs her ears, warm and velvety as they surely must be.

Annotated Bibliography

Andreasen, N. (2004, July/August). "Secrets of the creative brain." *The Atlantic*. Discount the "eureka" moment in creative thought. Nancy Andreasen describes creative work as, "...Newton's formulation of the concept of gravity took more than 20 years and included multiple components: preparation, incubation, inspiration—a version of the eureka experience—and production." Creativity in work and personal life is a long-term iterative process of trial and error to achieve the results we desire.

Andrews, T. (2005). *Animal speak: The spiritual & magical powers of creatures great & small*. Liewellyn Publications. Across cultures and over time in myths, legends, fables, and other verbal or written tales animals speak with humans. They deliver messages, often of divine origin, through behaviors we call animal medicine. Andrews describes the medicine of those we may encounter and how to understand the meaning animals offer to change our lives.

Arbinger Institute. (2010). *Leadership and self-deception*. Berrett-Koehler Publishers, Inc. We self-deceive because stories or patterns in our lives are not recognized. We are comfortable in our self-deception until we "Get out of the box," the authors say. Awareness is key.

Arrien, A. (2011). *Living in gratitude: A journey that will change your life*. Sounds True, Inc. Practice monthly exercises to live a grateful life. Negative thoughts disappear when we live in gratitude. Try to sing when you are angry.

Bell, J. (2014). *How to make a living as a writer*. Compendium Press. Practical recommendations for creative use of your abilities, time, energy, and resources to be a successful writer. Although Bell targets his book toward the writer who seeks to publish, practical advice for all writers and communicators is found in an easy-to-read, understandable format. Among my favorite recommendations is "Make an appointment with your desk." How do we become who we want to be unless we set aside time for ourselves?

Biesenbach, R. (2018). *Unleash the power of storytelling*. Eastlawn Media. Tell your story to "win hearts, change minds, and get results," says the author. Stories have captivated attention for millennia. Make your personal and business tales memorable when you follow basic steps of story creation and presentation.

Blanchard, K. (2017). *Self leadership and the one minute manager*. William Morrow. A fable of self-leadership for managers in an easy-to-read format. Leadership is depicted as a situational four-part model to direct, coach, support, and delegate.

Bolker, J. (Ed.). (1997). *The writer's home companion*. Owl Books. Support your writer's journey with the best works of writers. Trace the evolution of writing craft from project to process. Make your written words be about you.

Bradberry, T. and Greaves, J. (2009). *Emotional intelligence 2.0*. TalentSmart. Successful leaders will develop emotional intelligence (EQ) to build upon their education and experience to become leaders. In today's work environment, IQ must be supplemented with knowledge and acceptance of the emotional side of our work. This handbook tells you how to achieve better EQ.

Brown, B. (2012). *Listening to shame.* TED2012. https://youtu.be/psN1DORYYV0?si=vXHlTiRC1IEx1hkx. "Vulnerability is the birthplace of creativity, innovation, and change," according to Brown. When we are vulnerable and accept failure, we are creative.

Brown, B. (2012). *Daring greatly.* Avery. "The courage to be vulnerable transforms the way we live, love, parent, and lead," says Brown. When we dare to risk, we succeed or fail by daring greatly. Read "The Man in the Arena" speech by Theodore Roosevelt that starts on page one. Make big plans and execute greatly.

Buckingham, M. (2007). *Go put your strengths to work.* Free Press. Maximize your strengths to yield greater rewards than efforts you might take to improve your weaknesses. Follow six steps to achieve excellent performance.

Carson, E. (2018). *When the wisconsin river flowed east.* WisContext, Wisconsin Public Radio. https://pbswisconsin.org/news-item/when-the-wisconsin-river-flowed-east/. We look at what seems obvious and assume what we see has always been true. Then we change our perspective, look at new data, and turn our belief upside down.

Covey, S. (2004). *The 7 habits of highly effective people: Powerful lessons in personal change.* Free Press. Covey's "powerful lessons in personal change" are a go-to resource for self-leadership and presence. Most important for me are the "Time Management Matrix" and "Circle of Concern/Circle of Influence."

Crowley, M. (Ed.). (1953). *Writers at work: First series.* George;

Van Wyck Brooks. Crowley describes the writing process as, "There would seem to be four stages in the composition of a story. First comes the germ of the story, then a period of more or less conscious meditation, then the first draft, and finally the revision, which may be simply 'pencil work' as John O'Hara calls it—that is, minor changes in wording—or may lead to writing several drafts and what amounts to a new work."

De Bono, E. (1992). *Serious creativity*. Harper Collins. De Bono is a leading advocate of lateral thought, the ability to use creative ideas that come at right angles to our train of thought. Creativity is a process that may be learned and applied. Try "provocation" when you are stuck. Use recommended tools to develop creativity in your work and life.

Dias, B. and Ressler, K., First reported by Quinn, E. (2013). *Mice can inherit learned sensitivity to a smell*. https://news.emory.edu/stories/2013/12/smell_epigenetics_ressler/index.html. "Researchers have found that when a mouse learns to become afraid of a certain odor, his or her pups will be more sensitive to that odor, even though the pups have never encountered it." Mice inherit fear. What are the implications for humans?

Dufresne, J. (2003). *The lie that tells a truth: A guide to writing fiction*. W. W. Norton & Company. Understand the use of facts in support of truth. Learn the writer's process and excel in your craft when you follow practical exercises for creative writing. Truth is relative.

Eagleman, D. (2015). *The brain: The story of you*. Vintage Books. Presence is what we know, packed into now. The author says, "We take conscious credit for all our ideas, as though we've done the hard work in generating them. But in fact, your unconscious brain has been working those ideas—consolidating memories, trying out new combinations, evaluating the consequences—for hours or months before the idea rises to your awareness and you declare, 'I just thought of something!'"

Fontaine, W. (2021). "Why you should write about what you don't remember." Pagliarulo, R. and Talarico, D. (Eds.). *Getting to the truth: The craft and practice of creative nonfiction.* (1st ed., pp. 21-32). Books by Hippocampus. Brilliant examination of "factual truth" compared to what we remember, "emotional truth." The spin we put on the facts, our memories, reveals more about ourselves than the actual events in our lives. Similar to Gabor Maté's idea, emotional truth may be our trauma and not the precipitating event.

Forni, P. (2011). *The thinking life.* St. Martin's Press. The author provides ideas to reduce distractions and get back to thinking to solve problems. How are we present when we are constantly distracted?

Garrett, J. and Garrett, M. (2002). *The Cherokee full circle: A practical guide to sacred ceremonies and traditions.* Bear & Company. See Chapter 3 on "Being and Doing." Practice ceremony in all parts of your life.

Gelb, M. (1998). *How to think like Leonardo da Vinci.* Delacorte Press. Follow "seven steps to genius every day," recommends Gelb. When we understand our brain, learn from the masters, and follow the principles of creativity, we develop our creative selves.

Gilbert, E. (2015). *Big magic: Creative living beyond fear.* Riverhead Books. Gilbert says, "Creativity is sacred, and it is not sacred. What we make matters enormously, and it doesn't matter at all." Creativity is a lonely process. We work alone and maybe we're fortunate to receive spiritual guidance. "Art is a crushing chore and a wonderful privilege," says Gilbert. "The work wants to be made, and it wants to be made through you."

Gleick, J. (2008). *Chaos: Making a new science.* Penguin Books. Engaging seminal work on innovative directions in scientific study. We live in a less predictable world than imagined. Yet, patterns of existence repeat in scale and time. Foundational work on interdependence in our universe.

Goldsmith, M. (2015). *Triggers: Creating behavior that lasts.* Crown Business. Instead of stimulus or emotion and response, practice stimulus, feel, think, and response. Evaluate the impact of environmental triggers through reflection and thoughtful consideration of your actions. Reflection is key.

Goldsmith, M. (2007). *What got you here won't get you there.* Hachette Books. Twenty habits of star performers that contributed to their success will prevent further career advancement unless they shift their focus from "me" to "we." Successful leaders will learn self-leadership before they begin to manage others.

Goleman, D. (2005). *Emotional intelligence.* Bantam Book. Revolutionary work on importance of EQ compared to IQ. Self-leadership and the ability to lead others requires the application of EQ in business and life.

Gornick, V. (2021). *The situation and the story.* Farrar, Straus and Giroux. "Every work of literature has both a situation and story." Like Gabor Maté defines trauma as our reaction to an external event (the situation), the story we tell ourselves about an event may define who we are and possibly our life. When we recognize the story (awareness and presence), we have potential to change both.

Hanh, T. (1992). *Peace is every step: The path of mindfulness in everyday life*. Bantam Books. Compassion is a cornerstone for personal peace. With inner calm and mindfulness, we have potential to bring peace to the world.

Hill, L. and Lineback, K. (2011). *Being the boss: The 3 imperatives for becoming a great leader*. Harvard Business Review Press. When you develop yourself, team, and network, you will become a great leader. Follow author-described techniques to lead and give most of your effort to the development of yourself. Where do you spend most of your time? Probably not on yourself.

Jacobson, E. (2008). *Appreciative moments*. Tenacity Press. A primer to live in the moment and find appreciation in everyday events to enrich your personal and professional life. To appreciate is to find good even in bad.

Kahneman, D. (2011). *Thinking fast and slow*. Farrar, Straus and Giroux. Creativity comes from intuition and cognition. Kahneman describes intuition as our mental awareness of solutions based on beliefs and prior experience. Intuition comes first and could be described as a "flash of inspiration." Think of intuition as *lateral* thought, and consider cognition as linear thought. Balance both for creative work.

Klaas, B., (2024). *Fluke: Chance, chaos, and why everything we do matters*. Scribner. The author entertains and enlightens as he questions models of prediction and rational choice. "Everything doesn't happen for a reason," he says.

"We control nothing, but influence everything." Since "everything matters," presence is essential. Flukes may change the world, a family name, another family's beliefs, and instill compassion in myself.

Kleon, A. (2012). *Steal like an artist: 10 things nobody told you about being creative.* Workman Publishing Co., Inc. Creativity is fluid. When we borrow from others and make our work unique, we contribute to make the world better. In our digital age, the author suggests an analog workstation for ideas and a digital work area to produce what we create. Use paper, pencils, markers, and other tools of the artist to find our ideas. Use computers and digital equipment to translate our creations for use by others. Think of computers as left-brain assistance and artist tools as right-brain aids.

Klinkenborg, V. (2013). *Several short sentences about writing.* Vintage Books. Forget what you learned in school and focus on the reader's needs. "The problem most writers face isn't writing," the author says, "it's consciousness. Noticing. That includes noticing language." When we pay attention, we become aware. Awareness leads to presence.

Kushner, H. (2002). *Living a life that matters.* Anchor Books. Purpose and meaning in life are our most important rewards. Material achievements are secondary. Purpose and meaning give direction for a creative life.

Lamott, A. (1994). *Bird by bird: Some instructions on writing and life.* Anchor Books. Among the best references on writing and creativity. To get a writing project completed, proceed "bird by bird" until finished. A "shitty first draft" is where we all begin.

Lencioni, P. (2002). *The five dysfunctions of a team: A lead-*

ership fable. Jossey-Bass. A guide to recreate functional teams that includes establishing trust, embracing conflict, fostering commitment, creating accountability, and focusing on definable results.

Lewis, T., Amini, F., and Lannon, R. (2001). *A general theory of love.* Vintage Books. Our brains are linked with those closest to us. We feel the pain of others, especially through our limbic system that does not clearly define where my body ends and yours begins. Especially appropriate research for study of intergenerational trauma and legacy burdens.

Lopate, P. (Ed.). (1995). *The art of the personal essay: An anthology from the classical era to the present.* Anchor Books. A seminal resource on the art and craft of the personal essay. The author defines the personal essay, gives examples, and shows how the genre fits in the broader classification of creative nonfiction.

Maté, G., Maté, D. (2022). *The myth of normal: Trauma, illness & healing in a toxic culture.* Avery. Groundbreaking research and reporting on disease and western medicine's cure-all approach to healing. Our bodies react in unique ways to our environment. Authors define how we respond as the "wisdom of trauma," our coping mechanism. Trauma is how our body reacts to an external event and not the event itself.

Meadows, K. (2001). "The quiet memoir: Finding conflict in a "quiet" life." Pagliarulo, R. and Talarico, D. (Eds.). *Getting to the truth: The craft and practice of creative nonfiction.* (1st ed., pp. 33-43). Books by Hippocampus. Conflict is the central ingredient for a successful memoir, especially for lives without significant events (a "quiet life") to invoke severe trauma.

Menakem, R. (2017). *My grandmother's hands: Racialized trauma and the pathway to mending our hearts and bodies*. Central Recovery Press. Our bodies hold unhealed reactions to trauma that are passed from generation to generation. Just as we learn the effects of trauma from our ancestors, we may break the chain and release prejudice, racism, and other negative attitudes that hold us back. In so doing, we heal the future.

Mind Tools, Ltd. (1995-2010). *The mind tools e-book: Introduction to practical creativity.* https://www.mindtools.com, (pp. 185-208). This book explains two approaches to technical creativity: "programmed thinking and lateral thinking." Creativity tools for business and industry are provided with application for the personal creative arts. The authors show how to include lateral thought in our lives.

Newport, C. (2016). *Deep work: Rules for focused success in a distracted world*. Grand Central Publishing. Endless meetings, emails, and social media distract us from creative solutions for important problems. Open-office work environments, multi-tasking, and constant interruptions hold us back from productivity, the primary objective of deep work.

Patterson, K., et al. (2012). *Crucial conversations: Tools for talking when stakes are high*. McGraw Hill. The authors cover techniques to recognize important conversations and manage our interactions to reach goals desired by all. A must read before you have an important conversation with your boss, peers, employees, and friends, or with a significant other.

Pink, D. (2006). *A whole new mind*. Penguin Group. A balance of left- and right-brain thought is necessary to prosper in today's world. Careers that depend on left-brain cognition are easily outsourced. Right-brainers will lead us to the future with emphasis on design, story, symphony, empathy, play, and activities that give purpose and meaning to our lives.

Prager, D. (1998). *Happiness is a serious problem*. Regan Books. Prager says that all animals, including humankind, seek to avoid pain. Humans, however, look for more than the status quo. We want happiness. He begins with concepts about happiness, followed by obstacles to achieve joy. The author concludes with attitudes and behaviors that are necessary to live a happy life.

Pressfield, S. (2002). *The war of art: Break through the blocks and win your inner creative battles*. Black Irish Entertainment. The author explains internal conflicts we endure before we become creative. And we won't become who we want to be until we conquer our resistance to be creative and make peace with our fears. He identifies "the mother of all our fears as the fear of success. When we recognize external help to eliminate resistance to success, be it from gods, spirits, Muses, or the sub-conscious self, we move toward our calling...." A brilliant and inspirational guide to remove blocks to our creativity.

Quinney, R. (2024). *Who are we?* Borderland Books. Our past is our present. Each day we live our memories. Who do we want to be other than who we think we are? "Although our life is shaped by our mind, we are more than our thoughts," Quinney says.

Real, T. (2022). *Us: Getting past you & me to build a more loving relationship.* Goop Press. Relationships don't end because of fights. Relationships die due to lack of repair. When we resolve disagreements, we meet individual needs for the benefit of us.

Reynolds, M. (2014). *The discomfort zone.* Berrett-Koehler Publishers. Practice self-awareness at three levels of knowing. Use your brain to think about meaning, heart for emotions to relate with others, and gut to sense for survival. Explore head, heart, and gut for creative expression in all that you do. Push your limits. Find creativity at the border between comfort and discomfort.

Rico, G. (2000). *Writing the natural way.* Penguin - Putnam. Use visual patterns for creative writing. Rico explains how to use cluster diagrams, similar to mind maps, to break our consciousness and produce clear, comprehensive, and effective communications. Take risks for creative output.

Robinson, K. (2013). *Finding your element.* Viking Press. Discover your talents and passions to be in your "element," as described by the author. When we become our authentic selves, we live at our creative best.

Robinson, K. (2010). *Out of our minds.* Wiley. We become creative when we question what we learned in school and the value of information we receive from our culture. Follow exercises to develop creativity and apply your inner knowledge for betterment in work and life.

Ruiz, Don M. (1997). *The four agreements: A practical guide to personal freedom.* Amber-Allen Publishing. Follow four agreements with yourself: "...be impeccable with your word, don't take anything personally, don't make assumptions, and always do your best." A short, meaningful, and enjoyable book loaded with ideas that will improve your personal and work life. I resonate with "don't take anything personally."

Ruiz Jr., and Ruiz, Don M. (2013). *The five levels of attachment.* Hierophant Publishing. We are attached to beliefs and assumed outcomes that prevent achievement of our personal vision. We give permission to the words of others to hurt us and hold us back. Personal freedom is enhanced when we identify and release our attachments.

Scheer, L. (2014). *The writer's advantage.* Michael Wiese Productions. Master your genre with a strategic approach to define you as a writer. Your creative work will separate you from the competition. Identify and pitch what makes you and your product unique to successfully navigate today's competitive market.

Schwartz, R. (2021). *No bad parts.* Sounds True. We have "multiplicity of mind," says Schwartz. Parts of us hold divergent beliefs that drive unproductive behaviors. The "Eight Cs of Self" are characteristics of self-energy. When we are led by "Self," we manage conflicting parts, demonstrate self-leadership, and motivate others. For me, compassion, one of the Eight Cs, is my best entry to Self.

Scott, S. (2004). *Fierce conversations.* Berkley Books. "The conversation is the relationship," advises Scott. When we appreciate this connection, we move from blame of others to understanding our role in meaningful communications. Helpful advice for personal and career conversations.

Smith, P. (2012). *Lead with a story.* AMACOM. Replace PowerPoint presentations with story-based communications. We learn by example and apply knowledge through experience. Stories were told before we wrote words. Today's leaders and creatives who have responsibility to communicate business, community, or personal mission and vision will benefit. We remember stories.

Taleb, N. (2007). *The black swan: The impact of the highly improbable*. Random House. A seminal exploration of the idea of the unknown unknown. (We don't know, and we don't know that we don't know.) Author describes three characteristics of his Black Swan: An unpredictable event, with consequences for our planet, civilization, and individuals, and after the event has passed, we imagine reasons for the occurrence so we may be more comfortable with ambiguity. Because random events are infrequent and therefore unpredictable, we discount their impact. Yet, they shape our lives in both important and mundane ways. We ignore them at our peril.

Thiel, P. (2014). *Zero to one: Notes on startups or how to build the future*. Currency. What do you believe that no one else does? Your answer is the idea for a new venture. Monopolies foster creativity, raise cost, improve products, pass cost to market, and increase profits. Create a monopoly for your idea.

Wall, B. (2008). *Working relationships: Using emotional intelligence to enhance your effectiveness with others*. Davies-Black Publishing. Ask purposeful questions to staff, peers, and significant others about your performance. Wall provides exercises to use emotional intelligence to improve business and personal relationships.

Wallas, G. (1926). *The art of thought.* (publisher unknown) The author describes creative thought as a four-step process from idea to finished application. His process is recognized as foundational for other models of creative thought. Because creativity is a process, it may be learned and applied.

Webb, J. (1999). *Tunesmith: Inside the art of songwriting.* Hyperion. Must read for beginners and experienced songwriters and musicians. We all have what's required to produce the next big hit.

Whyte, D. (2001). *Crossing the unknown sea: Work as a pilgrimage of identity.* Riverhead Books. You are captain of your ship. Discover who you are at your core self and make your identity known. A poet for the business world, Whyte speaks a language of metaphor with story for what we do and who we are.

Acknowledgments

I am grateful to the following for their help in the preparation of this book: fellow writers and instructors at the University of Wisconsin-Madison Writing Center and the former Writers' Institute for ideas, encouragement, and revealing the muse; writers in formal and informal circles for review and feedback on blogs, essays, and parts of this book; friends and family for endless conversation on memories and drafts; Richard Quinney, friend and mentor, for support in photography, music, and publishing; Wayne Brabender, longtime friend, writing partner from 2017 (including twice-a-week writing days for over three years) for commitment to writing, discussion, genealogical research, and completing our books together; and Suzan McVicker, my wife and inspiration, for love, brilliance, and bringing writing into my life.

Thanks, also, to editors of magazines and journals who published these essays:

"Auditorium Host," *The Bookends Review* (2023).

"Dirty Bunny," *Unlimited Literature Magazine* (2022).

"Winner's Club," *Unlimited Literature Magazine* (2021).

"Found Money," *Hare's Paw Literary Journal* (2021).

About the Author

Richard W. Wilberg is an author, musician, photographer, creativity coach, and former business executive. He writes essays, creative nonfiction, songs, poetry, and self-development articles. He holds a BS degree from the University of Wisconsin-Milwaukee, an MS degree from Michigan State University, a Professional Coaching Certificate (PCC) from University of Wisconsin-Madison, and a Professional Certified Coach Certificate (PCC) from the International Coaching Federation. Richard lives with his wife, Suzan McVicker, in Middleton, Wisconsin.

Contact or follow Richard at:
   r_wilberg@yahoo.com
   www.rwilberg.com/contact/
   https://www.linkedin.com/feed/
   www.x.com/@r_wilberg
   https://richardwilberg.substack.com/
   https://soundcloud.com/richard-wilberg-music/

If you enjoyed this book, please leave a review on your favorite book website(s). Reviews are a great help to independent authors like Richard.

~ Thank you